MADE IN
HANFORD
The Bomb that Changed the World

MADE IN
HANFORD
The Bomb that Changed the World

HILL WILLIAMS

Washington State University Press
HILLSBORO PUBLIC LIBRARIES
Hillsboro, OR
Member of Washington County
COOPERATIVE LIBRARY SERVICES

Washington State University Press
PO Box 645910
Pullman, Washington 99164-5910
Phone: 800-354-7360
Fax: 509-335-8568
Email: wsupress@wsu.edu
Website: wsupress.wsu.edu

Library of Congress Cataloging-in-Publication Data

Williams, Hill, 1926-
    Made in Hanford : the bomb that changed the world / Hill Williams.
        p. cm.
    Includes bibliographical references and index.
        ISBN 978-0-87422-307-1 (alk. paper)
    1. Atomic bomb--United States--History--20th century. 2. Plutonium
industry--Washington (State)--Hanford--History--20th century. 3. Hanford
Wash.)--History--20th century. 4. Williams, Hill, 1926- 5. Pasco (Wash.)--Biography.
6. Pasco (Wash.)--History--20th century. 7. Atomic bomb--Social aspects--History--
20th century. 8. Nuclear weapons--Testing--Social aspects--History--20th century
    9. Nuclear weapons--Testing--Environmental aspects--History--20th century.
I. Title.
    QC773.3.U5W55 2011
    623.4'51190973--dc22

                                                                    2011006408

WSU PRESS

Fine Quality Books from the Pacific Northwest

On the cover: The underwater Baker nuclear
explosion, July 25, 1946, Bikini Atoll.
Courtesy of the Department of Energy.

*To Mary Lou, whose support and patience
helped make this project fun.*

Contents

Introduction

This book had been bothering me for quite a few years, almost an itch to get it written. I didn't help split the atom, do any of the engineering or construction at Hanford, and certainly didn't contribute to the mathematics or physics that went into the huge project. But I lived through—sometimes witnessed—important events at the beginning of the atomic age. It was something I wanted to share.

I tell the story in four parts:

- We first look at the immense transformation of the Hanford area from sleepy Washington farmland to a top-secret nuclear installation. This first part focuses on Hanford, which, after all, was only one of the major installations across the country in the massive project to build atomic bombs. But it was the one that mystified and then changed the Pacific Northwest, and the one I saw take shape near my hometown.
- Secondly, we look at the scientists who learned to split and manipulate the atom, identify and isolate plutonium, and take the first steps toward a bomb.
- In the third part, we salute the engineering that, seemingly against odds, transformed esoteric laboratory research into blueprints for factory buildings at Hanford. We consider the government's huge, secret gamble that Hanford would actually produce something.
- The book's fourth part concerns the intense nuclear testing that continued for more than a decade after the end of World War II, and how it disrupted the lives of people whose remote island homes were selected as targets. I saw the devastated islands where people had once lived, the deep craters where islands had

been blown out of existence by American super bombs. I am embarrassed now that it didn't occur to me to wonder about the people who had owned those ruined islands. But over the years I've talked to the people who left their ancestral homes to make way for the tests and have begun to realize the enormity of what happened to them when the atomic age arrived.

Most of the science and engineering at Hanford occurred before I got my first job as a reporter. Many of the people involved in the early years, perhaps feeling it was the most important work they'd ever done, wrote about their experiences. I have relied on those personal accounts.

One of the more interesting is the diary of Lt. Col. Franklin T. Matthias, the Army commanding officer at Hanford. Matthias's secrecy-obsessed boss, Brig. Gen. Leslie R. Groves, had forbidden the keeping of diaries on the project but relented if Matthias's was submitted to Groves's office for editing.

I was lucky to have access to a copy of Matthias's first draft diary. Mary B. Coney, now a professor emeritus of human-centered design and engineering at the University of Washington, interviewed the long-retired Matthias in 1991 regarding his work at Hanford. He lent her his original, unedited diary, a copy that Groves didn't know Matthias had kept for himself. Ms. Coney kindly lent me her copy, along with tapes of her interviews with Matthias.

The edited, official version of Matthias's diary is at the Department of Energy's public reading room in Richland. It is also currently online at reading-room.pnl.gov/edocs/matthias_diary.pdf.

This story leaned heavily on the memories of those who wrote about what they did and thought as they worked on the bomb, the Pacific Islanders who told me their stories, and the anthropologists who worked with them. To all of them, my heartfelt thanks.

And, finally, I appreciate the help of Henry Rukowski, a physicist and my Shoreline neighbor, who read the manuscript and offered helpful suggestions, and the staff at Washington State University Press—Glen Lindeman who retired recently as editor-in-chief, WSU Press Director Mary Read, Nancy Grunewald, Caryn Lawton, Patrick Brommer, and Kerry Darnall, my editor—who have been consistently enthusiastic and helpful.

—Hill Williams

Timeline

1932   February 27: James Chadwick announces his identification
        of the neutron.
        November 8: Franklin D. Roosevelt elected President of the
        United States.
1933   January 30: Adolf Hitler becomes Chancellor of Germany.
        March 12: First concentration camp opens outside Berlin.
        March 23: Enabling Act gives Hitler dictatorial power.
        Leo Szilard realizes a chain reaction might be possible.
1934   August 19: Hitler becomes Führer of Germany.
        Enrico Fermi unwittingly splits uranium atom.
1935   September 15: German Jews stripped of rights by Nuremberg
        Race Laws.
1936   February 6: Hitler opens the Winter Olympics in Bavaria.
        August 1: Hitler opens the Summer Olympics in Berlin.
1937   January 20: Inauguration of Roosevelt to a second term as
        U.S. president.
        May 12: Coronation of King George VI and Queen Elizabeth
        of England.
1938   March 12: Nazis annex Austria.
        November 9: Kristallnacht begins in Germany.
        December 24: Meitner and Frisch realize German scientists
        have split the atom.
1939   January: Niels Bohr travels to America with news about the
        Germans.
        September 1: Niels Bohr and John A. Wheeler predict Element
        94 (plutonium).
        September 1: Germany invades Poland, beginning World
        War II.

1940   April 9: Nazis invade Denmark and Norway.
        May 10: Winston Churchill becomes Prime Minister of Britain.
        May 10: Nazis invade France, Belgium, Luxembourg, and the
            Netherlands.
        May-June: Dunkirk evacuation of crushed British-French
            armies.
        September 7: German Blitz against Britain begins.
        November 5: Roosevelt elected to third term as U.S. president.
1941   January: Crucial mistake slows German bomb research.
        February 25: Plutonium isolated in California laboratory.
        December 6: American research on plutonium for bomb
            authorized.
        December 7: Japan attacks Pearl Harbor; America enters the
            war.
1942   June 18: U.S. Army Corps of Engineers initiates the Manhattan
            Project.
        August 7: American forces land on Guadalcanal.
        December 2: Nuclear chain reaction achieved at University
            of Chicago.
        December 22: Col. Matthias inspects Hanford site.
1943   January 16: Gen. Groves approves Hanford site.
        February 8: U.S. troops complete the conquest of Guadalcanal.
        February 26: Col. Matthias asks local editors for secrecy.
        March 22: Construction begins at Hanford.
        September 8: Italian surrender to Allies is announced.
1944   February-March: U.S. forces secure Enewetak and Bikini
            from the Japanese.
        June 6: D-Day in Europe.
        June 13: Germans begin rocket attacks on Britain.
        August 25: Liberation of Paris.
        September 20: At Hanford, B Reactor goes critical, quickly
            dies.
        December 16-27: Battle of the Bulge in the Ardennes.
        December 28: At Hanford, B Reactor finally reaches full
            power.

1945   February 3: First plutonium shipment leaves Hanford.
        February 4-11: Roosevelt, Churchill, and Stalin meet at Yalta
        Conference.
        February 19: Marines land on Iwo Jima.
        April 12: President Roosevelt dies. Harry Truman becomes
        president.
        April 23: Confirmation that Germany never tried to build
        an atomic bomb.
        April 30: Hitler commits suicide.
        May 8: VE (Victory in Europe) Day.
        July 16: First U.S. test of plutonium bomb in New Mexico.
        July 16: Potsdam Conference begins.
        August 6: Uranium bomb dropped on Hiroshima.
        August 9: Plutonium bomb dropped on Nagasaki.
        September 2: Japanese sign the surrender agreement;
        VJ (Victory over Japan) Day.
1946   February 10: Bikini people told their atoll is needed to secure
        peace in the world.
        March 7: Bikini people move from their atoll.
        July 1 and 25: Operation Crossroads nuclear tests at Bikini.
        August 6: Bikini leaders briefly visit Bikini Atoll.
1947   January 1: Atomic Energy Commission assumes control of
        the U.S. nuclear program.
        December: Enewetak people move from their atoll.
1949   August 29: Soviet Union tests its first atomic bomb.
1951   January: Nuclear testing site established in Nevada.
1952   November 1: Hydrogen bomb Mike detonated at Enewetak.
1954   March 1: Hydrogen bomb Bravo detonated at Bikini; fallout
        contaminates Rongelap Atoll and the people are taken for
        treatment.
1957   The Rongelap people return to their atoll.
1958   April 28: More than 20 nuclear tests over four month period
        begin at Enewetak.
        August 18: Nuclear tests end at Bikini and Enewetak.
        October 31: Unilateral cessation of nuclear tests announced.

1968 September: Community elders inspect Bikini.
1972 Replanting of coconut trees on Bikini largely complete; several
families return.
1975 High radioactivity levels force evacuation of Bikini.
1977 Cleanup of Enewetak begins.
1979 May 1: Marshall Islands become self-governing.
1980 October 1: Enewetak people reoccupy part of their atoll.
1982 The peoples of Bikini, Enewetak, Rongelap, and Utrik Atolls
file compensation claims with the United States.
1985 Rongelap is evacuated again due to remaining radioactivity.
1996 United States allocates $45 million to clean up Rongelap;
project is continuing.
2011 Marshall Islands claims still outstanding.

Part One

The Arrival

It was in this curiously low-key way that first word of the Hanford project arrived in Pasco, a project that would transform the town, the nation—and would change the course of history.

February 23, 1943

Hanford Area

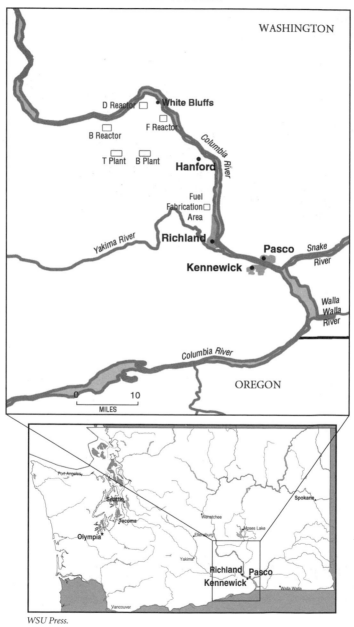

WSU Press.

Chapter 1

Secrecy

I n the old days, the flurry of a weekly newspaper going to press was followed by a quiet, relatively relaxed day. That would have been the way it was at the weekly newspaper in Pasco, a small town along the Columbia River in southeast Washington State, on the afternoon of February 26, 1943. The editor would have been catching up on paperwork, a printer dismantling columns of lead type, someone still cleaning up the mess of inky, crumpled papers from the night before. It was that kind of an afternoon when a young Army officer appeared in the *Pasco Herald* office and said he wanted to talk to the editor.

The officer, Lt. Col. Franklin T. Matthias, was new in town. He had arrived a few days earlier, probably by train because the nearest airline service in those days was at Pendleton, Oregon. And he probably arrived in the middle of the night because schedules of the old Northern Pacific Railway's fast trains were for the convenience of customers in the larger markets of Spokane and Seattle, and Pasco was between the two. The railroad telegraph would have been clattering away in the station, seemingly noisier at night when everything else was quiet.

That afternoon as Matthias walked toward the *Pasco Herald* office he may have passed the old J.C. Penney building where clerks still put customers' payments in tiny cash carriers that were whisked in pneumatic tubes to an unseen office upstairs where someone—we imagined a wizened man with thick glasses and pursed lips—did the paperwork and sent change zooming back down to the main floor.

I mention these details because my hometown of Pasco in early 1943 would have been much like towns across the country as America entered its second year of fighting after the attack on Pearl Harbor.

World War II had brought changes to the Pasco area. The Navy had built a flight-training base nearby, attracted by good flying weather all year. The Army was constructing a warehouse complex, already dubbed Big Pasco, to take advantage of rail connections to Seattle, Portland, and Spokane. There were sailors and soldiers on the streets. But overall, Pasco and the nearby towns of Kennewick, Richland, Hanford, and White Bluffs hadn't changed much for a long time.

The approach of spring 1943 was a hopeful time for both farmers and shopkeepers who were beginning to recover from the grim years of the Great Depression. Spring comes early to that basin and its farms and orchards were known throughout the state for first-to-market crops. Cherries, asparagus, strawberries, peaches, apples—all had fetched good prices the year before. Farmers and businessmen were looking forward to another good year.

But people in the towns and farms along the Columbia River that spring couldn't imagine how much their world was about to change.

It was a Friday when Matthias walked into the *Herald* office. As usual, press day at the weekly had run late the night before as individual sheets of newsprint, each the size of four pages, were fed by hand into the old flat-bed press, then turned over and fed through to print the other four pages, before a machine folded and cut them. The papers were addressed, bundled, and delivered to the post office for delivery in town and to catch the early-morning train that would drop them off at smaller towns throughout the county.

The editor, a lanky, 6 feet, 4 inches, unfolded from his desk chair to shake hands with Matthias, who showed identification as an officer in the Army Corps of Engineers and said he wished to discuss an issue of national importance. The young man's identification seemed authentic despite the civilian clothes so the editor motioned to a chair in his office. Matthias remained standing and asked that the office door be closed.

The whole thing must have seemed preposterous to the editor, a genial, relaxed 49-year-old who tended to find humor in unexpected places. Here was a stranger walking in off the street and announcing that he had information of national importance…in Pasco with a

Hill Williams Sr., editor of the *Pasco Herald*, feeds the press in this 1942 photo, a year before an unprecedented request that he not write about the nearby Hanford project. *Courtesy of the author.*

population of about 3,500 and a weekly newspaper, the *Herald*, of about 2,000 circulation, a typical small-town operation. In fact, its back room still contained, along with stacks of newsprint, a few bags of wheat used by cash-poor farmers to pay the $2 a year subscription during the Depression.

The editor was amused because the office partitions, about five feet high, weren't designed for privacy. However, he was also curious, so he closed the door and they sat down to talk. Matthias told him a secret project of utmost importance to the war effort would be built nearby. He gave no hint as to the nature of the project but said it would be huge and stressed again its importance to the war effort and the necessary secrecy.

It was in this curiously low-key way that first word of the Hanford project arrived in Pasco, a project that would transform the town, the nation—and would change the course of history.

Then Matthias, seated in the office chair, his head only slightly below the office partitions, made a startling request. He asked the editor's cooperation in not publishing news about the top-secret project. He probably mentioned that other papers and radio stations were getting the same request. In today's world it would seem extraordinary, asking a newspaper not to publish information about important work in its own backyard, a project that would be obvious to its readers and everyone else in the area, activity that would become a favorite topic of speculation.

Both Matthias and the editor knew the war had not been going well for America and its allies. Nazi Germany had conquered most of Europe and confronted Great Britain across the English Channel. German bombs were still occasionally pounding London, not yet recovered from the Blitz. The Japanese had significantly damaged the American Navy at Pearl Harbor, overrun most of Southeast Asia, and defeated American forces in the Philippine Islands.

At home the war had widespread popular support. Young men were being drafted into the armed forces but there were no anti-war demonstrations. Many families had husbands or sons on the battlefields. There was little complaint about wartime rationing of gasoline and tires and shoes. Housewives carried ration books when shopping for meat, coffee, sugar, canned food, or butter. (That week's *Pasco Herald* carried grocery ads listing food-coupon points as well as prices: Canned pineapple 16 points, 25 cents; baby food, 1 point, 8 cents.) The common attitude: If these inconveniences help the war effort, they're okay.

There must have been at least a brief silence in that tiny office— the door still closed—after the young colonel requested the news blackout. Not a standoff, but at least a silence. The colonel may have been thinking of recent British intelligence that German scientists were working on atomic energy, with a good possibility they had a head start on building a bomb. The editor would not have known about that and he undoubtedly had misgivings about suppressing news at the Army's request. But, despite worrying about the open-ended nature of the request, he told Matthias he would cooperate.

The contrast between the two men was interesting. Both had farm backgrounds, Matthias on a well-established family farm in northern Wisconsin, the editor on a dry-land homestead in the sagebrush country of central Washington. Matthias was a construction engineer with degrees in civil engineering from the University of Wisconsin. The editor had a degree from Washington State College (in those days still often considered "just" an agricultural college), had taught school for a few years, and then bought a half interest in the *Pasco Herald*. Matthias was in the ROTC in college, was commissioned a second lieutenant in the Army Corps of Engineers in 1930, and ordered to duty in April 1941. The editor had tried to enlist in the Army in World War I but was turned down because of a congenital heart defect that would kill him only five years after this meeting.

Matthias's diary mentions the meeting and that the editor agreed to cooperate, but gives no other details. Given the lanky editor's relaxed, laid-back nature, that he was in shirtsleeves and his tie probably loosened, the highly organized colonel may have written him off as a typical small-town editor in a place no one had ever heard of. And the editor? Well, he knew that promoters are drawn like flies to newspapers to ballyhoo their ideas. But this young man was asking for secrecy instead of publicity. Still, the editor tended to be skeptical of big ideas and probably wondered if this was another pie-in-the-sky project. However, he had agreed to the colonel's startling request and he intended to keep his word. He turned back to the more immediate business of getting out the next week's edition of the *Pasco Herald*.

Earlier that same day Matthias had obtained a similar promise from editors of the daily *Walla Walla Union-Bulletin*. A day or two later he visited the Yakima paper. Other officers talked to Ralph Reed of the *Kennewick Courier-Reporter*, across the river from Pasco, and to Robert Gay of the *Prosser Record-Bulletin*, up the Yakima Valley. Along with editors in Seattle, Portland, Spokane, and other cities in the region, they agreed to the troubling request to forego news coverage of a project that in normal times would rate banner headlines.

The editor of the *Pasco Herald* was Hill Williams Sr., my father. I was a senior at Pasco High School that year, trying to forget a disastrous basketball season, wondering if I should enlist or wait for the draft, and working after school at the *Herald*, like other papers suffering a wartime shortage of printers. I had no way of knowing my life would be touched—changed—repeatedly by a new science. I don't remember that my dad talked that evening about the Army officer's visit. I do remember in later months, as the enormity of the Hanford project became apparent, his good-natured grousing at the supper table that he was sitting on the biggest news story of his career and couldn't write about it.

Franklin T. Matthias
Department of Energy.

Matthias had set up a temporary office in Pasco four days before he visited the *Herald* office. Even though construction on the Hanford project would not begin for another month, he undoubtedly had a good idea of the enormity of the job ahead. But it's doubtful he suspected what else he would encounter in the next months— unhappy congressmen, residents infuriated at losing their homes and farms, concerns about the health of salmon or whether workers might get Rocky Mountain spotted fever from ticks in the sagebrush, an Indian tribe with fishing rights on the river, Navy flight cadets unwittingly wandering into Hanford's restricted air space, and other colonels and generals battling to protect their kingdoms from Hanford's insatiable demand for men and equipment. Plus he had a hard-driving boss with an uncanny ability to absorb and retain every detail and a habit of phoning at all hours to complain about lack of progress.

Matthias had "discovered" Hanford on December 22, 1942, almost two months before he appeared at the *Pasco Herald* office. The weather in the southeast corner of Washington was unseasonably mild that winter day, although snow and ice from an earlier cold spell still marked the top of Rattlesnake Mountain looming over the bleak plain sloping to the Columbia River.

As the 34-year-old Matthias looked over the wide-open country, his methodical engineer's mind reviewed a checklist of requirements—water, electrical power, enough land to accommodate huge plants that with luck would produce explosives for a new kind of bomb, isolated enough that if something blew up it wouldn't kill too many people.

The plants would produce plutonium, a word Matthias had first heard only a week before. He must still have been trying to adjust to the idea that huge—and destructive—amounts of energy can be liberated by splitting atoms.

It was a top secret trip. Matthias consulted only with military authorities and didn't even tell them what the land would be used for. He identified his two companions as civilian Army employees. Actually, they were engineers for the chemical giant E.I. DuPont de Nemours & Co., already selected to build and operate the plutonium plants.

The three men had been looking at possible sites for about a week. The requirements pretty much ruled out the built-up East Coast and the heavily farmed Midwest:

- A rectangle of land about 12 miles by 16 miles so the plants would be at least 20 miles from any town with a population of more than 1,000.
- At least 25,000 gallons per minute of water and 100,000 kilowatts of power.
- No main highway or railroad closer than 10 miles to one of the plants.
- And, for security, away from either coast and at least 200 miles from the Mexican or Canadian border (although, as it turned out, Hanford wasn't quite that far from Canada).

Matthias and the DuPont engineers, Gil Church and Allan Hall, had looked at sites in western Montana, central Idaho, and in eastern Oregon near the Columbia River. They had investigated a site southwest of the recently completed Grand Coulee Dam, considering the possibility of pumping water from the lake behind the dam to cool the plutonium plants. The dam had begun producing power about a year earlier.

On December 22, 1942, they flew over the scattered farms and three little towns along the Columbia River: Hanford, White Bluffs, and Richland. Forty years later Matthias remembered that his first sight of the Hanford area from the airplane impressed him as perfect for the plutonium plants.

He and the DuPont engineers also drove and walked around the area. Matthias, the construction engineer, sifted handfuls of the sandy, gravelly soil through his fingers. Rocky outcrops revealed that the sand and gravel were underlain by basalt bedrock. It was an ideal foundation for big concrete buildings.

A high-voltage power line linking Grand Coulee and Bonneville Dams ran through the site and a nearby substation meant power for construction would be available with little delay.

Matthias had been told to avoid not only heavily populated places but also farmland that produced food for the war effort. He described

Aerial view of prewar White Bluffs.
Department of Energy.

the Hanford country as barren, little developed, and with almost no people—a description that would have surprised the farm families on land homesteaded by their fathers or grandfathers.

Matthias's appraisal was understandable from a young man from the Midwest who had previously worked for the Tennessee Valley Authority and the Delaware Aqueduct project, all in populated, well-watered parts of the country. This was probably his first good look at the arid West. Farms and towns were buttoned up for the winter. In fact, some of the farms were temporarily deserted because the owners had taken advantage of winter, when farm work lessens, to take defense jobs over on the coast.

Even the season would have added to the deserted look of the land. Matthias's visit was the day of the winter solstice, the time of year when the sun stays as low as it ever does. If the sun was out at all, sagebrush and bunchgrass would have thrown long shadows on what, to a young Midwesterner, must have appeared an empty, weather-beaten, dismal landscape.

Matthias and the DuPont engineers were convinced Hanford was what they were looking for.

Matthias's boss, Brig. Gen. Leslie R. Groves, told them to check a couple of sites in southern California that turned out to be either too close to cities or lacking sufficient water. So on New Year's Eve, 1942, the three, back in Groves's Washington, D.C., office, unanimously recommended the Hanford area.

Groves himself took a look a couple of weeks later, on January 16, 1943, and approved it.

Leslie R. Groves
Department of Energy.

"I was pleased with the relatively small amount of cultivated land we would have to take over," Groves wrote later. "Most of the area was sagebrush suitable only for driving sheep to and from summer pastures in the mountains and even for that purpose could not be used oftener than once in several years. The total population was small and most of the farms did not appear to be of any great value…the distinct impression [was] that the owners were having a pretty hard time making them pay."

Groves stopped at a store in Hanford to buy crackers for lunch. The store's proprietor had little reason to suspect the cracker sale would be among his last. Or that the big, haughty, but carefully polite general—in civilian clothes on this trip—was on the verge of a decision that would close down the store and the town, take the proprietor's home and force him and his family and their neighbors to leave everything but their memories.

Groves was also pleased that "the site was well isolated from nearby communities, the largest of which was the town of Pasco, and if an unforeseen disaster should occur, we would be able to evacuate the inhabitants by truck."

Richland in 1942, population about 250.
Ralph Smith, U.S. Navy.

By truck? At the time, of course, Groves knew that the towns of Hanford and White Bluffs would be wiped out and that Richland would become an employee village, more easily managed than the typical small town. That left Pasco, population about 3,500, and the smaller Kennewick where there still had not been a hint of the momentous changes just weeks away, or any inkling that an Army general considered it feasible to load women, infants, children, teachers, older persons, railroad workers, farmers, patients at the hospital in Pasco as well as the nuns who ran the hospital—still in their long black habits in those days—into Army trucks and drive them off to some safe place.

Imagine soldiers trying to convince thousands of independent-minded residents of those small towns and farms they must immediately leave their homes and climb into trucks because of a danger they couldn't see or smell, was too secret to talk about, and which no

Richland in 1945, population 15,000.
Department of Energy.

An early favorite in Oregon

Even before Groves dispatched Matthias, the general had ideas about where to build the plutonium plants based on his earlier assignments in the West and suggestions from other officers. A site in Oregon along the Columbia River was at the top of the list. Groves described it as "the most likely prospect...about 30 miles south of the site finally chosen at Hanford." But it had been taken over by the Army Air Corps in 1941 as a precision bombing range and, Groves said, to have forced out the Army "would have drawn undue attention to our work."

This area is still known as the Boardman Range, across the Columbia River from Washington. It had much the same characteristics as Hanford: near the river, plenty of space, available power from Bonneville and Grand Coulee Dams, isolation, and a small population.

So, except that the Army had first dibs on the Boardman site, the plutonium factory might have been in Oregon.

one had heard of anyway. Fortunately, it never became necessary. The process of making plutonium did release radioactive material to the atmosphere, more than the government admitted for 40 years. But the downwind residents didn't know and there was never an order to herd them into trucks.

As a colonel with the Army Corps of Engineers, Groves had supervised construction of the Pentagon, which was nearing completion in 1942. He had been promised a combat command in North Africa, a good path for promotion. Instead, in September 1942, he was told he would head the Manhattan Engineer District, the nondescriptive name for the top-secret attempt to develop atomic energy for weapons of war.

The disgruntled Groves found himself heading two programs, both aimed at building a bomb in time for use in the war, but by different methods. One that would utilize uranium was already transforming a sleepy Tennessee valley near Oak Ridge into a huge manufacturing complex. The other part of the Manhattan Project was based on the hope—little more than hope at that time—that the man-made element plutonium, isolated only a year before, could be produced in large enough quantities to make a bomb, and that such a bomb would actually be possible. The plutonium program, almost an afterthought in the Manhattan Project, was getting a later start than the work in Tennessee.

The plutonium factory originally had been planned for Tennessee. But making plutonium on a large scale was new, untried, and potentially risky—very risky. In Tennessee the plutonium plants would have been about 15 miles from Knoxville, a city of more than 100,000 in 1942. The search turned to the wide-open spaces in the West.

Groves knew at the time he sent Matthias looking for a site that the plutonium project was a huge gamble. In fact, a month earlier when he was trying to convince a reluctant DuPont to take on the project, he realized he was asking the company to accept "a hazardous, difficult and perhaps impossible undertaking."

Still irritated at missing the coveted overseas assignment, Groves asked for a status report from Col. Kenneth D. Nichols, who was the second in command in the Manhattan District and who himself had been with the project for only a few weeks. Groves's irritation turned to dismay. "In fact, I was horrified," he wrote later. "It seemed as if the whole endeavor was founded on possibilities rather than probabilities."

Groves, who had just turned 46 when he became head of the Manhattan District, was one of the more complex, sometimes infuriating, characters in the nation's rush to build the bomb.

Disliked by many fellow officers even before he became head of the Manhattan District, he immediately demanded a promotion to brigadier general because "I felt that my position would be stronger if they [the atomic scientists] thought of me as a general" instead of a colonel. The demand was bumped up to Gen. George C. Marshall, Army chief of staff, who, because of the project's top priority approved by President Franklin D. Roosevelt himself, okayed the star for Groves.

Vincent C. Jones, who wrote the Army's official history of its part in the Manhattan Project, commented caustically that Groves "seems not to have considered that for several months...other officers had been dealing successfully with project scientists in spite of their relatively low military rank."

Groves's grab for a general's star was only one of the reasons he was thoroughly disliked by fellow officers. He stepped on toes, he bruised feelings, he ignored the chain of command. His was a domineering personality, impatient with delay and—particularly—incompetence. He was a man who harbored deep suspicions, who had undying dislikes but also lasting loyalties. But he could whip projects into shape and get things done. Some doubt the bomb would have been completed for wartime use if Groves had not been in charge.

Groves's number two man, Col. Nichols, later wrote: "First, Groves is the biggest SOB I have ever worked for. He is most demanding. He is most critical. He is always a driver, never a praiser. He is abrasive and sarcastic. He disregards all normal organizational channels. He is extremely intelligent. He has the guts to make timely, difficult decisions. He is the most egotistical man I know." Nichols's written memories seem to pause, as though the author were taking a deep breath. Then he added: "If I had to do my part of the atomic-bomb project over again and had the privilege of picking my boss, I would pick General Groves."

Matthias reminisced 40 years later that "Groves was an overbearing type of guy, but if he liked someone, he was pretty decent. If he had confidence in people, they couldn't do anything wrong."

Matthias had impressed Groves as a skillful problem-solver during construction of the Pentagon. And on December 14, 1942, a week before Matthias first saw the Hanford country and not long after DuPont had reluctantly agreed to take on the plutonium project, Groves had sent the colonel to Wilmington, Delaware, to sit in on a meeting with DuPont scientists. The general told Matthias to act "solely as an observer." The implication that he keep his mouth shut probably wasn't difficult for Matthias that day. At that point he didn't know much more than that it was a huge, secret project.

When Matthias returned to Washington early the next morning, he was surprised to find Groves waiting at the railroad station to give him a ride home. Generals don't usually offer rides to lieutenant colonels. Groves used the 20-minute drive to brief Matthias on the purpose of the plutonium project. As the car stopped at Matthias's home, the colonel remarked with a wry grin that he would need to re-read Buck Rogers, the science-fiction character then featured in a comic strip and radio show. The colonel's skills and interests were heavy construction, not nuclear physics.

Before Matthias got out of the car, Groves told him to start that very day on a study of possible sites for the plutonium plants. That was December 15, 1942, eight days before Matthias and the DuPont engineers "discovered" Hanford. Under Groves's relentless prodding the plutonium project was being pushed into fast forward.

Matthias may have considered it another temporary assignment. But a few weeks after Groves's visit to Hanford, probably late January or early February 1943, he called Matthias into his office. Matthias remembered Groves telling him, "I have been told I can have any Corps of Engineers officer I want to run the Hanford project, anyone not tied up in a combat assignment…I wish you'd check around and give me some recommendations."

Matthias nodded and started for the door when Groves added, "And by the way, if you don't find anybody I like, you're going to have to do it yourself." Matthias recalled that he considered for a moment and then said, "'General, there isn't anyone I can recommend.' So he appointed me right then."

It wasn't long after that seemingly offhand appointment that Matthias began calling on newspapers with the extraordinary request that editors stifle news instincts for perhaps the biggest story of their lifetimes, not for a few weeks or months but indefinitely. Secrecy had been clamped on the entire project, secrecy with an iron hand.

Hanford Main Street, late 1930s.
Department of Energy.

White Bluffs Main Street, 1940.
Department of Energy.

Chapter 2

The Neutron: A New Tool

N ot long after Hill Williams Sr., editor of the *Pasco Herald*, had agreed to an extraordinary Army request to sit on the biggest news story of his life, he got another unexpected request, almost a demand: That he open his home to strangers.

The DuPont Company, which had agreed to build and operate the Hanford plants, desperately needed living space for thousands of workers. Construction workers and their families would be housed in a temporary village near work sites, but DuPont's white-collar force, chemists and engineers, was already on the way and within days would need to be housed. Eventually, they would be able to bring their families to new houses in Richland. But in the spring of 1943, those houses were still in the planning stage.

Representatives of DuPont asked many homeowners in the area to make room available to the newcomers. One approached the editor, probably calling him "Mr. Hill" because people often got his name backward. The appeal was mostly to patriotism because of the importance of the secret war project. But everyone realized there simply was not enough hotel space in the area.

The editor, my father, felt that our family of five—including my mother, my two younger sisters, and me—pretty well filled our home. However, it seemed the patriotic thing to do and we did have a spare room, the one we called Grandma's room for when she visited. My parents reluctantly agreed but with the stipulation that "they be nice people."

So, along with others in Pasco and nearby Kennewick, as well as towns up the Yakima Valley, our family took in strangers. Ours were Mr. Carter and Mr. Lee, both lonely for their families in Wilmington, Delaware (DuPont headquarters). A few months later when I joined the Navy, my room was occupied by a third renter, Paul Nissen, a civilian employee of the Army Corps of Engineers who had the impossible job of trying to keep Hanford speculation out of newspapers while keeping newspapermen happy—or at least not too unhappy.

We had no idea what Mr. Carter and Mr. Lee did during the day. And they themselves may not have known that their jobs were contributing to a terrible new weapon that would end the war, lead to a 40-year standoff with the Soviet Union, and influence world events for the rest of our lives.

Our family probably was typical of others in America, unknowingly facing the change from a familiar past to the frightening world of atomic energy—and weapons. My parents had grown up on farms in wheat country. As a girl, my mother would rise before dawn to make pies for the harvest crew's big noon meal. My dad, in summers during college, drove a team of horses pulling a harvester that cut and bundled stalks of wheat—expertly maneuvering to avoid tipping over on steep hillsides in the Palouse country. Like most Americans in the spring of 1943, we were ignorant of recent advances in atomic research and of America's suddenly energized program to build an atomic bomb.

Unnoticed by many Americans, the atomic clock actually began ticking for Hanford only 11 years before construction of the plutonium factory started. In February 1932, James Chadwick, a shy, quiet British scientist, announced his discovery of the neutron, a subatomic particle that would become the tool to split atoms and produce plutonium at Hanford. It seems a logical place to begin the story of the science that catapulted the tiny town of Hanford to world notice.

News of Chadwick's neutron discovery probably didn't make much of a public splash in 1932. It would have been difficult to think of everyday uses. But it was of intense interest to the small group of scientists who had slowly been learning the structure of the atom.

This is what was known by the time Chadwick began looking for the neutron, some 80 years ago: Almost all of the atom's mass is in a tiny nucleus that itself is composed of positively charged particles called protons. The nucleus is surrounded by mostly empty space

James Chadwick

James Chadwick identified the neutron in 1932 and helped develop the plutonium bomb.
Public domain.

In many ways, James Chadwick fit the old science-fiction stereotype of a scientist working in a musty laboratory: tall, thin, a high domed forehead over a sail-like nose, horn-rimmed glasses, quiet, shy. So shy, in fact, that as an 18-year-old entering college intending to study mathematics, he mistakenly got in the registration line for physics. Too shy to admit his mistake, he signed up for physics classes. He disliked them at first but was soon engrossed.

As a 23-year-old graduate student he was studying in Berlin in 1914 and was interned as an enemy alien when World War I began. He spent four years at a racetrack converted to a prison, sharing with five other prisoners a stall originally built for two horses. Chadwick used equipment given him by his German teachers to conduct experiments during his prison time and even gave lectures to fellow prisoners. One story says he used German toothpaste containing thorium (advertised in those innocent days as a tooth whitener) as a radioactive source in his experiments. The war years left him with lifelong stomach problems he blamed on the prison diet of "war sausage made from bread soaked in blood and fat."

and electrons (negatively charged particles). The charges of the protons and electrons cancel each other so the atom itself has no charge. Hydrogen, the lightest element, has one proton. Uranium, the heaviest element then known, has 92 protons. The periodic table listed the known elements from No. 1 hydrogen to No. 92 uranium.

But there was a puzzle. Except for hydrogen, with one proton and a mass of one, the masses of the atoms didn't agree with the number of protons. For example, helium with two protons has a mass of four and uranium with 92 protons has a mass of 238.

We now know, of course, that the extra mass is accounted for by neutrons bound with protons in the nuclei of all elements except hydrogen. Neutrons have no electrical charge, a characteristic that made them difficult to detect and to understand.

Chadwick was aware of French and German experiments that had produced a stream of high-energy particles, a new and intense form of radiation with a remarkable ability to zip unimpeded through solid matter. The radiation was created by bombarding beryllium, a metal, with particles emitted by a radioactive source such as polonium. When this mysterious radiation was directed at hydrogen-rich paraffin, it actually knocked protons out of hydrogen atoms. But no one could identify the new kind of radiation.

Chadwick repeated the German and French experiments, directing the mystery stream of particles against a lump of paraffin, achieving the same result. To understand what he did, think of a game of billiards, an explanation Chadwick sometimes used. He was using the mystery particles as cue balls fired at atoms in the paraffin. Most of

Weight and mass?

What is the difference between weight and mass? Weight, also called gravitational mass, describes the force of gravity on an object. Mass, or inertial mass to physicists, refers to how much a given force will accelerate an object and depends solely on how much matter is in the object. Example: An object with a mass of one kilogram on Earth would still have a mass of one kilogram on the Moon. But it would weigh only one-sixth as much because of the lower gravitational force.

the particles went right through the paraffin without hitting anything. But, just as in real billiards when the cue ball smacks into a game ball and sends it flying, some of the particles struck protons and knocked them out of hydrogen atoms. Calculating the energy gained by these displaced protons, Chadwick concluded the mystery radiation must consist of particles with no electrical charge and a slightly greater mass than protons. He named them neutrons.

The discovery that neutrons are clustered in the atomic nucleus along with protons answered the puzzle of why the masses of atoms do not match their numbers in the periodic table. For example, the helium nucleus has two protons and two neutrons for a mass of four. The uranium nucleus, with a mass of 238, contains 92 protons and 146 neutrons. (Electrons have such small mass they make only a negligible contribution to the mass of the atom.)

But as soon as physicists realized the nucleus of the atom is composed of protons and neutrons squeezed together, they faced other puzzles. If you add up the total mass of the protons and neutrons in a nucleus, the total is slightly more than the mass of the nucleus itself. The parts are more than the whole. It's as though you put two pounds of apples and two pounds of oranges together on a scale and they weighed slightly more than four pounds.

Other questions the physicists faced were just as puzzling. If neutrons have no electrical charge, what holds them in the nucleus with the protons and why don't they just fall out? If protons are all positively charged, why do they stick together in the nucleus? Playing with magnets tells us that like charges repel each other. You'd think the protons would repel each other and cause the nucleus to fly apart.

As it turned out, Albert Einstein had provided the answers. One of the predictions in his 1905 paper on special relativity was that mass and energy are different forms of the same thing—that mass can be converted into energy and vice versa. So the "missing" mass in the nucleus was not really missing at all. It was the energy binding the protons and neutrons together, the amount of energy that would be required to break the nucleus into protons and neutrons. And it is the energy released if the nucleus is disrupted (i.e., if the atom is split).

Discovery of neutrons was an important step toward understanding atomic structure. Still, it's doubtful that Chadwick or others realized immediately that the discovery would change history. Surely no one realized in 1932 that the discovery put an irrevocable hold on a tiny town named Hanford in a remote patch of desert nearly 5,000 miles from Chadwick's laboratory. However, scientists at the time were intrigued with the question of whether the binding energy released when the nucleus is disrupted could be utilized for power generation or even ship propulsion.

Ernest Rutherford, director of the Cavendish Laboratory where Chadwick worked, had actually knocked a proton out of a nitrogen nucleus in 1919. Even the newspapers noticed that "atom splitting" achievement. But Rutherford concluded the "energy in" was so great that the "energy out" wasn't worth the effort. His "cue balls" were alpha particles, two protons and two neutrons bound together, essentially the nucleus of a helium atom. Because the particles were positively charged, he could accelerate them to high velocity. But the closer the positively charged alpha particles approached the positively charged nucleus, the stronger they were repelled. So the energy required to accelerate the particles to a speed where they could actually strike the nucleus made it a massive undertaking.

In fact, London newspapers reported that Rutherford, at a scientific meeting in 1933, had dismissed discussions of commercial power from splitting the atom as "talking moonshine." Given the tools he had available, his pessimism was understandable.

Think about the neutron, a tool Rutherford did not have when he split the nitrogen atom. The neutron is fast moving, not repelled or even affected by electrical fields. Researchers quickly realized it would be ideal as an atomic probe—penetrating, like a bullet, through the atom. Most would pass right through, of course, but if a neutron struck a nucleus head-on, it could knock something loose. That idea led to further speculation: If the neutron can break up an atom's nucleus and send protons spinning out of place, might it also dislodge other neutrons? And might those dislodged neutrons smack into and disrupt other nearby nuclei, knocking loose even more neutrons in a

Leo Szilard, brilliant and eccentric, contributed ideas to the bomb project.
Argonne National Laboratory.

self-sustaining process—releasing a large quantity of the binding energy that had held things together?

One of the first to think about that possibility and its implications was a 35-year-old Hungarian scientist in London, a Jewish refugee from Hitler's Europe. It was in 1933, just one year after Chadwick's discovery of the neutron, when Leo Szilard was out walking on a misty morning in London. He had read newspaper reports of Rutherford's pronouncement that talk of power from splitting atoms was "moonshine." Szilard said later the story set him thinking as he walked.

He had stopped at a red traffic light, he said, and "as the light changed to green and I crossed the street, it…suddenly occurred to me that if we could find an element which is split by neutrons and which would emit *two* neutrons when it absorbs *one* neutron, such an element if assembled in sufficiently large mass, could sustain a nuclear chain reaction. I didn't see at the moment just how one would go about finding such an element, or what experiments would be needed, but the idea never left me."

The idea of obtaining almost unlimited power from splitting atoms was a radical concept in the 1930s when most energy was derived from chemical reactions—burning wood, coal, oil, or gasoline. Even the release of energy in a TNT explosion is a chemical reaction. None of these changes the atom's nucleus.

When Rutherford broke up the nitrogen atom, a tiny amount of energy was released. But when he ended the experiment and the bombardment of alpha particles stopped, the nuclear changes stopped. For atomic energy to be put to large-scale use, the chain reaction must be self-sustaining, must continue without outside help. It would work only if an impacted nucleus absorbed a neutron "cue ball" and emitted two or more neutrons, and if those neutrons disrupted other nearby atoms. In the 1930s no one knew if that was possible. But in Szilard's later years, he often recounted his sudden insight as he crossed the street in London in 1933.

Szilard, newly arrived in England in 1933, had worked with Einstein in Germany and would have been familiar with the implications of Einstein's 1905 paper—that energy and mass are different forms of the same thing. In fact, Szilard and Einstein had collaborated for years in Berlin trying to develop, of all things, home refrigerators without moving parts. They even invented and patented the so-called Einstein-Szilard pump for the project but the development never got off the ground.

It's unclear whether Szilard in 1933 was thinking of a chain reaction in terms of commercial power or of a weapon with great destructive power. But within a few years, driven by the fear that Hitler's scientists would be first with an atom bomb, he became an important contributor to Britain and America's efforts. Yet after Germany's surrender and the widespread assumption that Japan was not working seriously on an atomic bomb, Szilard joined other scientists in an unsuccessful campaign against dropping the bomb on a Japanese city, suggesting instead a warning drop in an uninhabited area.

Chapter 3

Minds that Shaped History

T he woman's black winter clothing was stark against the snow as she walked briskly alongside a younger man striding on cross-country skis. She was talking earnestly; he was listening but not as earnestly. He wanted to talk about something else.

But the woman persisted, describing surprising, puzzling information. Finally, the man slowed and began to listen seriously—then with increasing disbelief.

It was the day before Christmas, 1938, in a small town near Sweden's coastline. Today that conversation is remembered as a crucial step toward harnessing atomic energy—and tightening history's grip on Hanford.

The letter that Lise Meitner, 60, a refugee from Nazi Germany, showed to her nephew on that winter day was from Otto Hahn, a researcher in Berlin who was asking for her help in understanding the results of a puzzling experiment. Hahn had actually split the uranium nucleus but didn't understand what had happened. He had written for help to Meitner, his long-time colleague before she fled Nazi persecution earlier that year.

In the 1930s, there was increasing interest in exploring the atomic nucleus, but it was still a quiet academic activity largely out of the public eye and involving only a few hundred scientists worldwide, most of them in European laboratories. Quiet, maybe, but exciting to the scientists involved.

Meitner had been Hahn's colleague at the Kaiser Wilhelm Institute in Berlin for 30 years, a brilliant member of the team. Because she had been born a Jew, she was forced to flee Germany on July 13, 1938, even though she had become a Lutheran as a young woman. At the Dutch border, a German guard asked to see her passport, which had

From left, Fritz Strassmann, Lise Meitner, and Otto Hahn in 1956.
University of California, Lawrence Berkeley National Laboratory.

expired 10 years before. As she held her breath, he studied it, handed it back, and waved her through. Perhaps the guard was inattentive or perhaps he didn't really want to stop refugees fleeing the Nazis. At any rate, Meitner resumed her work in Sweden, but isolated and without the excellent laboratory equipment of the institute in Berlin.

Meitner and Hahn had been using neutrons to bombard the uranium nucleus at the time she fled. Now, a few months later, Hahn had written Meitner about mystifying results of a similar experiment he and Fritz Strassmann had performed. He was frankly asking for help.

As Hahn and Strassmann, both chemists, had analyzed the results of the bombardment, their expectations were guided by conventional wisdom of the time—that the nucleus of an atom, a tiny cluster of protons and neutrons, behaved as a solid particle. At best, they thought a colliding neutron might knock a proton or two out of the uranium nucleus. If that happened, the remaining product would be an element close to uranium in size and mass.

Instead, their analysis—and they were world-renowned chemists—seemed to reveal the presence of barium, an element with 56 protons in its nucleus, not much more than half the size of uranium's 92 protons. They couldn't bring themselves to believe it. In fact, based on experiments by Irene Curie in Paris a few months earlier, they were expecting radium, which has 88 protons in its nucleus, fairly close to uranium's 92

Hahn wrote to Meitner: "The fact is, there is something so odd about the 'radium isotopes' that for the time being we are telling only you about it…Our 'radium' isotope is behaving like barium…Perhaps you can suggest some kind of fantastic explanation." Notice that Hahn indicated his doubts by putting the word radium in quotation marks.

As Christmas approached friends had invited Meitner to join them for the holidays in a tiny resort town near the coast. Meitner traveled there from Stockholm a few days before the holiday and her nephew, Otto Frisch, 34, also a refugee from Germany, came from Copenhagen to join her for a few days.

Frisch, a physicist like his aunt, finally read the letter from Hahn. "Barium. I don't believe it. There's some mistake," he exclaimed. Indeed, it would have seemed impossible to almost anyone in 1938 that even speeding neutrons could knock that big a piece from the uranium nucleus. Nothing larger than protons had ever been knocked out of the nucleus. And now, almost half of a 92-proton nucleus? Frisch was understandably skeptical.

Meitner insisted that Hahn was too good a chemist to have made an obvious mistake and, as Frisch recalled, the pair sat on a log in the snowy landscape to discuss it. In a curious twist of history, Frisch worked at the Copenhagen laboratory headed by the great Danish physicist Niels Bohr. So Frisch was familiar with a radical idea Bohr had suggested just two years earlier: that the atomic nucleus behaves in much the same way as a liquid drop, rather than as a solid particle. The new concept would change the approach to nuclear research. But Hahn and Strassmann may not have heard of it or, more likely, dismissed it.

As Meitner and Frisch, sitting on the log, speculated how a squiggly uranium nucleus might deform when impacted by a neutron, Meitner pulled paper and pencil from her purse and they began drawing sketches. Frisch finally came up with a sketch of a nucleus shaped like a dumbbell—he called it a circle squashed in the middle.

If a neutron struck and was captured by a squiggly uranium nucleus, they speculated, the added energy could cause the nucleus to become unstable and deform—into a dumbbell shape—and finally split into two separate pieces. Frisch later borrowed the word fission from biology to describe the process.

Hahn's letter had said: "We understand that it can't break up into barium…So try to think of some other possibility."

We know now, more than 70 years later, that Hahn's experiment indeed had split the uranium nucleus, with 92 protons, into barium, 56 protons, and krypton, 36 protons. But the combined mass of the two was less than that of uranium. The "missing" mass had been converted to energy.

On that wintry day, two superbly prepared minds affected the course of history. Frisch quickly calculated the force driving the two fragments apart—two clusters of protons in opposite ends of

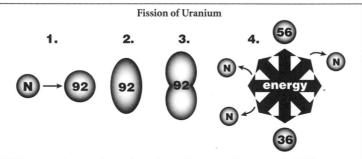

Fission of Uranium

(1) A neutron impacts the nucleus of a uranium atom (92 protons). (2) The energy of the impact disturbs the nucleus and, acting somewhat like a liquid drop, it begins to deform. (3) The nucleus may assume a shape where clusters of positively charged protons begin repelling each other, overcoming the force holding them together. (4) The uranium nucleus splits, releasing the energy that had held the protons in the nucleus, and splitting the uranium nucleus into barium (56 protons) and krypton (36 protons), and releasing two or three neutrons.

the dumbbell repelling each other. His result was the equivalent of 200 million electron volts. While seemingly impressive, that's a tiny amount of energy—but it is the result of splitting one atom, and there are a million trillion atoms in one gram (1/28th of an ounce) of uranium.

They wondered about the source of that much energy. Meitner knew how to calculate the mass defects of nuclei (the difference in mass between the parts and the whole). She quickly determined it would amount to one-fifth the mass of one proton—minuscule. But, as Frisch pointed out, that tiny amount of mass, applied to Einstein's formula (energy equals mass multiplied by the speed of light squared) came out to 200 million electron volts. "So here was the source for that energy," Frisch recalled. "It all fitted."

It was a fateful moment for civilization. One wonders if there was a stunned silence as aunt and nephew sat side by side on the log.

The holiday over, Frisch returned to Copenhagen, eager to tell Bohr of the letter from Hahn, and of his and Meitner's speculation about the idea of a wobbly nucleus deforming into a dumbbell shape and breaking apart. Frisch recalled years later: "I had hardly begun to tell [Bohr] when he struck his forehead with his hand and exclaimed: 'Oh what idiots we have been. Oh, but this is wonderful. This is just as it must be.'"

Bohr left a few days later for the United States for a stay at the Institute of Advanced Study at Princeton University. He brought to America the momentous, sobering news that Germans had split the uranium atom. It was a time when nuclear research in the United States was still a relaxed, uncoordinated, underfunded effort carried out mostly in university laboratories.

Meitner, Frisch, and Bohr realized that when the uranium nucleus divided, it would release two or three neutrons as the newly created elements achieved stability. It had been five years since Leo Szilard's insight as he crossed a London street that if an element could be found that emitted two or more neutrons after being split by one neutron, a nuclear reaction could be sustained.

Szilard recalled in later years that he wondered which elements might emit two or more neutrons for each neutron captured. "The reasonable thing to do would be to investigate systematically all the elements," he wrote. Regarding himself a thinker rather than an actual experimenter, however, he considered it a boring job to investigate all 92 known elements. "So I thought that I would get some money… and then hire somebody who would just sit down and go through one element after the other."

Szilard couldn't interest anyone in providing the money and the "boring" job fell to a group of young Italians in Rome.

About four years earlier, Enrico Fermi, who was in his early 30s, had begun the ambitious task that Szilard had thought about. It was probably late in 1933 when Fermi learned that Irene Curie and her husband Frederic Joliot had induced radioactivity in aluminum. The Paris team had used alpha particles as projectiles, a method that required massive amounts of energy.

Fermi decided neutrons, identified by James Chadwick only about a year earlier, would be more efficient projectiles. Being not only a thinker but also an enthusiastic laboratory technician, he began with hydrogen, the lightest element, and began working up the list of elements. He was awarded a small grant (less than $1,000 in today's money) from an Italian agency and enlisted friends for help. By today's standards, it was a bare-bones project—Fermi built his own Geiger counters. One member of his team, Emilio Segrè, recalled visiting apothecaries and chemical suppliers in Rome searching for seldom-used chemicals—and paying cash.

It was pioneering work. Fermi's group bombarded 60 elements and produced radioactivity in 40 of them. Their work was of immediate interest to scientists because it showed that artificial elements could be created easily and in the quantities required for further study. Previously, such work required expensive equipment such as the cyclotron, developed a few years earlier in America.

By accident, Fermi's group made a discovery that represented another step toward a plutonium bomb. Most of the tables in Fermi's lab were topped with stone, but there were several wooden tables.

The technicians were puzzled that the target materials became more radioactive when bombarded on the wooden tables than on the marble-topped tables. Fermi wondered if the wood might be having an effect on the neutrons. They tried other materials to "filter" the neutrons—paraffin and even water in a goldfish pond out in back of the lab. The results were dramatic. Radioactivity increased in the target materials as much as 100 times when the neutrons were directed through paraffin or water.

"Everyone was summoned to watch the miraculous effects of the filtration by paraffin," Segrè recalled. "At first I thought a counter had gone wrong because such strong activities had not appeared before."

Enrico Fermi
Argonne National Laboratory.

Despite the excitement, Fermi said it was time for lunch and went home. By the time he returned to the lab later that day he had a possible answer: The "filters" were indeed affecting the neutrons. They were being slowed down by collisions with hydrogen nuclei, each nucleus consisting of one proton, in the wood, the paraffin, and the water. Because neutrons and protons are almost the same mass, the collisions were as effective in slowing neutrons as the cue ball is slowed in billiards collisions. Fermi concluded that slow-moving neutrons are more likely to be captured by nuclei in the target material, explaining the increases in radioactivity. It was counter to the accepted belief at the time that fast neutrons would be the most effective. The neutron "filters" came to be called moderators, common in modern reactors.

Finally, as Fermi and his group bombarded one element after another, they came to uranium. The results were puzzling. The bombardment seemed to have produced new man-made elements beyond uranium, never before known. When their work was presented at a scientific meeting, it was a sensation. Newspapers ballyhooed the new "transuranic elements."

Fermi was uncomfortable with the news coverage. He himself was in doubt about what he had found. The so-called "transuranic" elements didn't show the expected characteristics.

As it turned out, he and his crew were wrong. They had actually split the uranium nucleus—probably the first to do it—but didn't realize it. The "transuranic" elements they thought they were seeing were actually fission products created as the uranium nucleus split, short-lived radioactive elements rather than any new, man-made elements beyond uranium.

Fermi's work was about four years before Hahn and Strassmann hit a similar blank wall and asked Meitner for help in interpreting their puzzle. Like most scientists at the time, Fermi considered that the atomic nucleus behaved as a solid particle. Conventional wisdom was that neutron bombardment might chip a small piece—a

Slow neutrons?

How slow are slow neutrons? Relatively speaking, very slow. Energy lost in collisions slows them to about 1.4 miles per second. The lesser energy—and speed—makes them more easily captured by atomic nuclei.

By comparison, fast neutrons are produced by fission (when an atom splits). Their greater energy can be translated to a speed of about 8,700 miles per second.

proton—from the nucleus. If that happened, the electrical charge of the atom—the number of protons in the nucleus—would change, as would the atomic mass. Logic said it would be a small change and that was what Fermi was looking for.

He would have known that Ernest Rutherford had knocked a proton out of the nitrogen nucleus, changing it into a form of oxygen that is nearly the same mass as nitrogen and only one number apart from it on the periodic table. Rutherford's experiment may have been in Fermi's mind as he tried to understand what had happened when he bombarded uranium with slow neutrons. He expected and tested for elements near uranium in the periodic table. He didn't look for elements that were only about half the size of uranium.

Segrè wrote in his biography of Fermi that "We proceeded to show that uranium irradiated with neutrons did not produce any elements with atomic numbers between those of lead and uranium." Lead is number 88 in the periodic table, fairly close to uranium at 92.

"The possibility of fission, however, escaped us," Segrè wrote, "although it was called specifically to our attention by Ida Noddack who sent us an article in which she clearly indicated the possibility of interpreting the results as splitting of the heavy atom into two approximately equal parts."

Noddack, a German chemist, was 38 when she published a scientific paper—and sent Fermi a copy—criticizing the interpretation that he had created elements beyond uranium. She suggested that Fermi might have actually split the uranium nucleus into several large fragments that would not necessarily be neighbors of uranium and that he should have looked farther down the periodic table instead of just between lead and uranium. Noddack apparently was the first to suggest the possibility of fission—two years before Bohr proposed the liquid-drop model of the nucleus, four years before Meitner and Frisch theorized how the nucleus could split, four years before the process was named fission. And four years before Fermi won the Nobel Prize for work that neither he nor the judges understood completely.

Despite Noddack's brilliant previous work—she and her husband Walter had discovered the element rhenium in 1925—her criticism of Fermi's work was ignored. We can assume it was at least partly because she was a woman, and a chemist rather than a physicist. And she was far, far ahead of her time.

Fermi had been embarrassed by the newspaper ballyhoo about elements beyond uranium and undoubtedly was further irritated by Noddack's sarcastic reference to "reports found in the newspapers" about his work. For whatever reasons, Noddack was ignored.

"The reason for our blindness is not clear," Segrè wrote many years later.

Noddack, who had suspected the truth, was nominated for the Nobel Prize several times for other work but never received it.

Otto Hahn, however, did win the Nobel Prize for chemistry in 1944 for "discovery of the nuclear fission of atoms." Hahn did not participate in Germany's unsuccessful program to make an atomic bomb but was taken into custody by the British, with other nuclear scientists, as the war neared an end. He and others were in "gentlemen's custody" in England in 1945 when he learned that he had won the Nobel Prize the year before.

Meitner was not mentioned in Hahn's award. Her exile to Sweden isolated her from many scientists and Hahn himself apparently never publicly credited Meitner for her contribution to his work. What many Meitner supporters felt was a "Nobel mistake" was partly remedied in 1966 when Meitner, Hahn, and Strassmann won America's prestigious Enrico Fermi Award.

Fermi won the Nobel Prize in 1938 "for his demonstrations of the existence of new radioactive elements produced by neutron irradiation, and for his related discovery of nuclear reactions brought about by slow neutrons." Still, neither he nor the judges realized he had split the uranium atom.

Meitner, whose insight helped explain the fission of uranium, was invited to join the British team preparing to go to America to help build the atomic bomb. She turned it down. Friends quoted her as saying she hoped the bomb project would fail, but feared it would be successful. Some opined that Meitner, a front-line nurse during World War I, had seen enough suffering and death. She spent the war in Sweden.

Despite Meitner's efforts to distance herself from the bomb, the American press gave her the celebrity treatment when she visited after the war, inaccurately calling her the woman who "left Germany with the bomb" in her purse. She died in 1968 in England.

Fermi went on to spearhead the scientific effort to build America's plutonium bomb. Someone once asked if he regretted missing the key discovery of fission in 1934. He replied: "I was eternally grateful I failed in making this discovery because if I had, I think the Germans and Italians would have been able to start the war with an atomic bomb instead of us ending it with one."

Part Two

The Science

"…the neutron is practically the theme song of this whole project."
The Smyth Report, August 12, 1945

Reactor team from the University of Chicago.
Back row, from left: Norman Hilberry, Samuel Allison, Thomas Brill, Robert Nobles, Warren Nyer, and Marvin Wilkening. Middle row: Harold Agnew, William Sturm, Harold Lichtenberger, Leona (Woods) Marshall Libby, and Leo Szilard. Front row: Enrico Fermi, Walter Zinn, Albert Wattenberg, and Herbert Anderson.
Department of Energy.

Hanford depot, late 1930s.
Department of Energy.

Chapter 4

Developing Fission

C onstruction of Grand Coulee Dam was big news in the 1930s for a Pacific Northwest in the grip of the Great Depression. A crowd of 1,000 watched as the first construction bids were opened in Spokane on June 18, 1934, and broadcast on the radio. It was a rare sign of hope.

Jobless men from across the nation were already heading for the Columbia Basin, lured by the promise of work on what was to be the biggest manmade structure on earth, displacing the Great Pyramid of Giza. Critics on the East Coast ridiculed the dam as a make-work project and wondered who would buy the power.

As the dam rose, schools took busloads of children to see what was billed as the "Eighth Wonder of the World." My Pasco eighth-grade class made the trip—boys on one weekend, girls on the next—and on the way home camped at a nearby state park.

The most direct route to the dam from Pasco, although not the fastest, went along a narrow, partly graveled road past a tiny town named Hanford, across the river on a ferry, and on to where the dam was rising.

It didn't occur to us or anyone else that the dam, the great river, and the wide-open country around Hanford would coalesce in late 1942 when the Army came looking for a place to make plutonium for bombs.

By January 1939, the dam was still three years away from generating power, and the river's flow had been lifted only a few feet as it tumbled over low concrete blocks at the beginning of the spillway. But across the country in that same month, the Danish scientist Niels Bohr stepped off a ship in New York carrying news that would electrify nuclear researchers—and change the meaning of the word Hanford.

Niels Bohr
Public domain.

It had been only a couple of weeks since Bohr had slapped his forehead and exclaimed, "Oh, what idiots we have been…This is just as it must be." Bohr was preparing to leave his Copenhagen laboratory for America when Otto Frisch excitedly told him that he and his aunt, Lise Meitner, believed German scientists had split the uranium atom, a previously unthinkable accomplishment.

Bohr, 53, arrived in New York on January 16, 1939, with an assistant, Leon Rosenfeld, a 35-year-old Belgian scientist. Rosenfeld remembered that Bohr told him as they boarded the ship, "I have in my pocket a paper that Frisch has given me which contains a tremendous new discovery, but I don't yet understand it. We must look at it."

Although Bohr was marginally seasick during the rough, nine-day crossing, his stateroom must have resembled a classroom with Bohr pacing, talking, writing on a blackboard, proposing ideas, using Rosenfeld as a sounding board, the way he taught classes at home. By the time they arrived in New York, Bohr had concluded that the Meitner-Frisch idea was a good start in explaining the theory of nuclear fission (atom splitting).

A star-studded reception party greeted Bohr as the ship arrived. Enrico Fermi, who had defected to America with his family after receiving the Nobel Prize a few weeks earlier, was there with his wife.

John A. Wheeler, a 27-year-old American who had studied for a year with Bohr in Copenhagen five years earlier, had arrived from Princeton where he was in his first year as an assistant professor of physics.

Bohr must have been dying to share the new idea with Fermi, who had actually split the uranium atom five years earlier but still hadn't realized it. But he didn't, hoping that Meitner and

John A. Wheeler
University of Texas.

Frisch would get credit for their discovery before the exciting news spread.

Bohr stayed in New York a day or two to visit the Fermis. Rosenfeld joined Wheeler on the train back to Princeton. Because neither was aware of Bohr's concern about priority for Meitner and Frisch, "Rosenfeld spilled the beans to me on the train," Wheeler recalled. "I was excited. Here was a whole new mode of nuclear behavior that we had overlooked."

Wheeler arranged for Rosenfeld to report the work at a meeting of physicists at Princeton that very evening. In an understatement, Wheeler remembered the Rosenfeld talk "caused a stir."

The listeners—researchers, faculty, and students—understood immediately the importance of Rosenfeld's report. He wasn't just talking about knocking a proton out of the nucleus, just knocking off a small chip. Instead, the "unbreakable" nucleus had, literally, been split in half. They would have been familiar with Einstein's work and realized that splitting atoms would release energy, possibly great amounts of energy.

That night it's doubtful they were thinking of chain reactions and atom bombs. More likely they were thinking of new research opportunities that would arise from the discovery and the chance to learn more about nature's basic structure. They were undoubtedly eager to get to their laboratories to see if they could duplicate the work.

Today, news of such a spectacular discovery would spread quickly across the country and around the world. But in 1939, it took nine days just for the news, in Bohr's head, to cross the Atlantic to America.

Perhaps even more important, most Americans, still struggling in the tough times of the Great Depression, were not aware of nuclear research in Europe and were not prepared for the news. Einstein was a familiar name then, but most people wouldn't have been sure what he had done and what, if anything, it had to do with splitting the atom.

There were a few newspaper stories as Bohr discussed the discovery at meetings in Washington, D.C., and at Columbia University in New York in the first weeks of 1939. One of them in the *San Francisco Chronicle* led to the oft-told story illustrating the intense excitement among scientists over the news of fission. Luis Alvarez, a professor at the University of California's Radiation Laboratory, was getting a haircut on campus when he saw the item. Supposedly, Alvarez abruptly jumped out of the barber chair (perhaps with the barber's cloth still over his shoulders) and literally ran to the Radiation Laboratory where he breathlessly blurted the news to Phil Abelson, his graduate student. By the next day, Abelson had achieved fission in his laboratory.

"It may seem odd that only days were required to confirm [fission] when it had taken years of painstaking work to discover it," Wheeler wrote. "The very energy of the fission process is what made it easy. Neutron bombardment was already an art practiced at numerous laboratories. Once physicists knew what they were looking for, it was short work to find a uranium target, set up the right detector and measure the characteristic large energy pulse of a fission event."

William L. Laurence, a *New York Times* reporter, was at Columbia University when both Bohr and Fermi explained the discovery of fission. Laurence, 50, not only understood what they were talking about but realized its importance. His story in the *Times* the next day reported that the energy liberated in splitting the uranium atom was "the greatest amount of atomic energy so far to be liberated by man on earth…the most important step yet made by science toward…the utilization of the vast stores of energy locked up within the nucleus of the atom."

If the scientists at the meeting talked of harnessing atomic energy for weapons, Laurence's story did not mention it. Likely they didn't. They were probably thinking of experiments and what they might reveal.

Despite the scientific excitement, Bohr realized the need of an explanation of how and why fission occurred. He asked Wheeler to work with him. To other scientists, it must have seemed an unusual choice—a 27-year-old American instead of Bohr's assistant Rosenfeld or older, more experienced physicists who had worked in Europe. Bohr obviously had been strongly impressed when Wheeler studied under him in Copenhagen five years before.

They made an interesting working pair. Bohr, 53, could lose himself in thought. His students in Copenhagen told how he would miss his stop on the trolley, go to the end of the line, get on a return car—and then forget to get off at his stop again. Wheeler, the young American, was undeniably bright. He had taught himself calculus in high school, had entered Johns Hopkins University at 16 and completed his doctorate in physics while he was 21. Like Bohr, he loved to teach and was good at it.

Both were theoreticians who spent more time working out problems in their heads than in laboratories. And, in the opinion of scientists who knew them, Bohr and Wheeler attacked problems in similar ways. Both needed solitary thought time broken by intense discussions where they would scribble formulas on a blackboard. (At the end of a session, Bohr would kick bits of chalk under a rug to avoid being scolded by the janitor.) Sometimes, they would aimlessly walk the halls, talking and questioning as they walked.

As they walked or jabbed at the blackboard, they agreed that the added energy of a neutron capture could deform the uranium nucleus significantly and cause it to fission.

Wheeler explained it this way: When you cut an orange in half, the two halves fall apart. This is not true of a nucleus. Suppose you could cut a uranium nucleus into two hemispheres. The powerful, short-range attractive forces that bind the protons and neutrons together would prevent the two halves from separating. But if the nucleus absorbs a neutron, the added energy will deform the nucleus, perhaps from the shape of an orange to that of a cucumber, then to a peanut—to a point that exceeds the short range of the attractive forces. At that point, the repulsive force of the positively charged protons would force the halves apart with great energy.

"Once the nucleus has acquired just enough extra energy [from the captured neutron] and is deformed into just the right shape…it comes 'unglued' and its parts separate, blown apart by their mutual electrical repulsion," Wheeler explained.

Although a nucleus that absorbed a neutron could lose the extra energy in several ways, Wheeler and Bohr concluded an excited

The model of the atom

The model of the atom as envisioned in 1939 remains basically valid today: A tiny positively charged nucleus of clustered protons and neutrons, surrounded by negatively charged electrons—equal to the number of protons—and mostly empty space. Research in the late 1960s and early 1970s established that both protons and neutrons are composed of still smaller particles known as quarks.

uranium nucleus "is more likely to undergo fission than to do anything else."

As Bohr and Wheeler worked out the process of fission, other experimenters at Princeton encountered a puzzle while bombarding uranium with neutrons. High-energy (fast) neutrons caused uranium nuclei to fission. But as the energy of the neutrons dropped, the likelihood of fission also dropped, until low-energy (slow) neutrons again caused fission in the uranium. It was Bohr who came up with the answer. It had been known since 1935 that uranium contains a tiny amount (0.7 of one percent) of an isotope, which is still the same element (No. 92 on the periodic table) but with three fewer neutrons:

Natural Uranium (U-238)	Uranium's Isotope (U-235)
92 protons	92 protons
146 neutrons	143 neutrons
238 (atomic mass)	235 (atomic mass)

Bohr reasoned that the cross section of the U-238 nucleus must increase with high-energy neutrons. (Physicists use the term "cross section" to describe a nucleus's probability of capturing a neutron. The bigger the cross section, the greater probability of absorbing a neutron and fissioning. It's like shooting at a barn door; the bigger the door the more likely you'll hit it.)

Bohr concluded that the increased fission with slow neutrons must be caused by the rare isotope, U-235, with a cross section that increases with lower-energy neutrons. Studying the fission process for U-235, Bohr and Wheeler realized that when U-235 fissions and stabilizes, it necessarily must release extra neutrons. It meant U-235 would be capable of creating a chain reaction—and releasing huge amounts of energy. "This line of reasoning led us to consider what other nuclei might be subject to fission by low-energy neutrons," Wheeler wrote. "We could predict with some confidence which isotopes of other elements, known or unknown, would also undergo fission under low-energy neutron bombardment."

Bohr and Wheeler predicted that a still-undiscovered element, two steps up the periodic table from No. 92 uranium, would be fissionable. They referred to it only as 94, its predicted place in the table. Element 94 was discovered two years later, but didn't get a name, plutonium, until a year after that.

What are isotopes?

Isotopes are different forms of the same element. An example is hydrogen. The nucleus of the common form of hydrogen is one proton. The nucleus of a hydrogen isotope, deuterium, has one proton and one neutron. Tritium, another hydrogen isotope, has one proton and two neutrons. They have different atomic masses—hydrogen 1, deuterium 2, tritium 3—but all are the same chemical, still No. 1 on the periodic table.

The nucleus of the most abundant form of uranium, No. 92, has 92 protons and 146 neutrons for an atomic mass of 238. The fissionable isotope of uranium still has 92 protons but only 143 neutrons for an atomic mass of 235. Uranium-238 and uranium-235 are the same chemical, both No. 92 on the periodic table and each with 92 electrons, and are chemically indistinguishable.

Curiously, neither Bohr nor Wheeler initially realized the implications of their Element 94 prediction. Another Princeton researcher, Louis Turner, pointed out that 94, when and if discovered, would be a different chemical than No. 92 uranium, meaning it could be separated from uranium by chemical methods.

The way an atom behaves in a chemical reaction is determined by the number and arrangement of its electrons. The predicted Element 94 atom would have 94 electrons, two more than No. 92 uranium, meaning the two elements would behave differently in chemical reactions and, thus, probably could be separated by chemical means. Turner's insight ultimately led to the massive plants at Hanford where plutonium, produced from uranium in reactors, would be separated from the uranium in a series of chemical reactions.

That same year, 1939, Albert Einstein, Leo Szilard, and Eugene Wigner, all refugees from Nazi Europe and suspecting that Germany was researching uranium, had convinced President Franklin D. Roosevelt to establish a uranium committee. It would investigate the possibility of an atomic weapon utilizing the uranium isotope U-235. But the possibility seemed slim. Because U-235 and U-238 are the same element, both 92 on the periodic table and both with 92 electrons, they are chemically indistinguishable. Separating out the rare isotope seemed almost impossibly difficult. But if 94 were discovered, separating it from No. 92 U-238 should be possible. Looking back, Turner's insight was game changing.

Bohr returned to Denmark, leaving Wheeler to apply finishing touches and prepare illustrations to their report. "The Mechanism of Nuclear Fission," detailing their explanation of the fission process and concluding that U-235 was likely responsible for slow-neutron fission, was published September 1, 1939—the day Germany invaded Poland, the beginning of World War II. Among interested readers, it was learned later, were scientists in Berlin. It was one of the last published reports on nuclear research before American and British scientists began withholding information that might benefit Nazi Germany.

A few days later, a newly appointed chemistry instructor at the University of California at Berkeley, Glenn T. Seaborg, 27, noted in his journal that he had read "an extensive and extraordinary article" by Bohr and Wheeler and "I intend to digest it." Two years later Seaborg was one of the discoverers of the predicted Element 94.

Glenn T. Seaborg discovered plutonium in 1941.
University of California, Lawrence Berkeley National Laboratory.

Chapter 5

Element 94

The February 25, 1941, entry in the laboratory notebook was calm, matter-of-fact: "It is now clear that our alpha activity is due to the new element with the atomic number 94." The newcomer, too small to be seen under a microscope or weighed, revealed its presence only by its radioactive signature, the "alpha activity."

But the young scientist who made the entry was anything but calm. "We felt like shouting our discovery from the rooftop," Glenn T. Seaborg remembered. And it really was worth shouting: discovery of a man-made element would eventually win a Nobel Prize. It was also a step toward a super bomb, another chapter in a story that would transform the world.

Working at the Radiation Laboratory of the University of California at Berkeley, Seaborg, 29, and Arthur C. Wahl, 24, a graduate student, had isolated what we know as plutonium, two steps above uranium on the periodic table.

Today, such an important discovery would be announced almost immediately, but even with America still at peace in early 1941, scientists studying the energy locked in atoms were voluntarily keeping quiet about their work. In fact, a year earlier when other researchers at Berkeley had discovered—and announced—Element 93, the first transuranic (beyond uranium) element, the British had protested publication of a potential military secret. Element 93, neptunium, was not suitable for weapons work. But the British were already at war with Germany and feared the Nazis had a head start on an atomic bomb, so they were supersensitive about any publication of fission research.

Element 94 was different. "We were aware from the beginning that...element 94 could be very important," Seaborg said. Even before it was officially discovered, scientists had predicted that 94 would be fissionable, similar to uranium-235, and possibly useful in a super bomb.

So by the time 94 was discovered, the usual sharing of scientific information had stopped. Seaborg reported the work to the Uranium Committee, a secret (and strangely inactive) government panel investigating the possibility of a uranium bomb. To establish priority, he sent a brief notice to a scientific journal, requesting it not be published because of government secrecy.

I will use the word plutonium here, but the new element was known simply as 94 until Seaborg named it about a year later. After that, those inside the huge secret project may have used the word. The public, however, even many of those working at Hanford, did not see or hear the word plutonium until after the bombs were dropped on Japan.

Let's consider exactly what the researchers at Cal's Radiation Laboratory had accomplished: They had confirmed earlier suspicions that when natural uranium (U-238) is bombarded with slow neutrons, some of its atoms will absorb a neutron. The extra neutron increases the uranium atom's mass by one, forming U-239, still atomic number 92. But U-239 is unstable and, through a process called beta decay, one of the neutrons decays into an electron and a proton. The electron is emitted while the proton remains in the

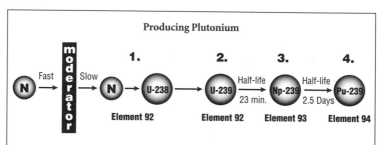

Producing Plutonium

A neutron is slowed by a moderator and (1) is absorbed by an atom of uranium-238, increasing its mass to 239 and destabilizing it. (2) The unstable U-239 emits a particle and decays to (3) neptunium-239 which, in turn, decays to (4) plutonium-239.

WSU Press.

Naming plutonium

Seaborg followed tradition when he named plutonium about a year after its discovery. Uranium, discovered in 1789, had been named for the planet Uranus, discovered eight years earlier. Neptune, the next planet farther from the sun, gave Element 93 the name neptunium. Pluto, still considered a planet in 1942, had been discovered in 1930 so Seaborg called Element 94 plutonium. By naming rules, it should have been plutium but Seaborg thought plutonium sounded better.

nucleus, increasing the atomic number to 93. But the new element, neptunium, is also unstable. Again through beta decay, it becomes Element 94—plutonium.

So, in extremely simplified terms and ignoring complicated and tedious laboratory work, if you bombard natural uranium with slow neutrons, nature takes over and in a couple of steps produces plutonium. Uranium-239, the first step, has a half-life (the time it takes for half of it to decay to neptunium-239), of about 23 minutes. And neptunium-239 has a half-life, during which half of it decays to plutonium, of about 2½ days. The transformation from uranium-239 to plutonium is practically complete in about two weeks.

This finding was tremendously important even beyond its pure scientific value. It came at a time when America's investigation of the feasibility of atomic weapons, half-hearted at best to that point, was on the verge of being dropped. Most scientists who knew about the work doubted an atomic bomb could be ready in time for use in the war almost everyone expected. The doubt is understandable. Early in 1941, the only likely explosive to make an atom bomb was uranium-235, the rare fissile component of natural uranium ore. The task of separating U-235 from the more abundant U-238 seemed overwhelming. Only tiny amounts of U-235 had been produced in laboratories. No one knew whether enough could be produced for a bomb or even how much would be needed.

The discovery at Berkeley revealed what seemed to be a simpler, faster route to a super bomb. If you bombard U-238 with slow neutrons and are patient enough to wait a while, the process produces plutonium. And there was also this: U-238 had been considered a useless byproduct of the tedious extraction of U-235, which comprises less than one percent of uranium ore. The Berkeley discovery that U-238 was a source of Element 94 multiplied, in effect, uranium's potential material for a bomb by almost 100 times. Admittedly, the plutonium created in this two-step process would still be mixed with uranium and a lot of nasty and dangerous byproducts. But No. 94

Emilio Segrè worked with Enrico Fermi in Rome in the 1930s and later with Glenn Seaborg at Berkeley.
University of California, Lawrence Berkeley National Laboratory.

was a different chemical than uranium, so it should be possible to separate and purify it by traditional chemistry.

The discovery moved Hanford one step nearer its inevitable emergence to worldwide prominence, although those of us living near Hanford in 1941 had no knowledge of what was going on.

Practical questions remained about 94. Would it turn out to be fissionable, as predicted? If so, would its fission rate be fast enough to sustain an almost instantaneous chain reaction, a super explosion? Would 94 be stable or, like 93, decay radioactively into something else so quickly it would not be usable?

As Seaborg tackled those questions, his team had been joined by Emilio Segrè. Segrè had worked with Enrico Fermi in Italy in the 1930s when they had actually caused uranium to fission without realizing it. As a recent immigrant, Segrè was not authorized to know about 94's chemistry. It led to "some absurd situations," Seaborg wrote. Seaborg would provide the chemicals and give Segrè instructions without telling him what he was doing. If Segrè had wanted to spy, Seaborg admitted later, it would have been easy for him to figure it out.

The hocus-pocus with Segrè matched the difficulties of working in labs equipped for the old rather than the new science. Needed equipment was in separate buildings and occasionally they carried radioactive samples across a street and up two flights of stairs to another lab. It must have been quite a sight as Seaborg and Segrè, wearing goggles and lead-impregnated gloves, scurried between buildings with irradiated uranium "in a lead bucket that we carried precariously on a long pole," Seaborg recalled.

After more work to make a larger sample of 94 (still too small to be visible, only about half of a millionth of a gram), Seaborg placed it against an instrument that detected fission pulses. "The counter registered the unmistakable kicks indicating fission," Seaborg wrote. And its fission rate was faster than that of U-235. He considered it "the moment of truth…not only for us personally but for the world."

More tests estimated 94's half-life at about 30,000 years, making it much more stable than U-239's half-life of 23 minutes. In actuality, 94's fission rate was a little less than they estimated, but still faster than U-235's, and the half-life turned out to be about 24,000 years. The numbers were pretty close for first estimates, although Seaborg modestly said later that was probably due to a "great number of errors we made [that] somehow, conveniently, canceled each other out."

"This fission rate was momentous news—element 94 would in fact be better than uranium," Seaborg wrote. "And the half-life was certainly long enough for it to be used for nuclear power, a bomb or other applications."

The discovery of Element 94 at Cal's Radiation Laboratory jolted America's nuclear research, until then an uncoordinated, scattered, and largely underfunded effort. Prospects for a uranium bomb seemed dim. With the tedious laboratory methods available in 1941, it would have taken thousands of years to separate enough U-235 for a bomb, even if anyone knew how much it would take—which they didn't.

Seaborg's group had a huge impact on the bomb program. Seaborg's boss, Ernest O. Lawrence, director of Cal's Radiation Laboratory, fired off an excited memo to a National Academy of Sciences committee that had been studying the uranium problem. Members had been on the verge of recommending that atomic research be dropped in favor of work on weapons with more immediate payoff.

Lawrence's memo pointed out that U-238, previously considered a useless byproduct after removal of U-235, actually could be a source of Element 94, a bomb material. He added, "If large amounts of Element 94 were available it is likely that a chain reaction with fast neutrons could be produced...at an explosive rate which might be described as a 'super bomb.'"

Lawrence, a member of the National Academy of Sciences uranium committee, would have been aware of work underway at Columbia University in New York, work that would turn out to be another step in the search for ways to produce the "large amounts of Element 94" he mentioned in the memo. But it would take a while.

In fact, in December 1940, Lawrence had talked shop with Enrico Fermi, the man who had unwittingly split the atom in Italy and by 1940 was at the physics department at Columbia University in New York City. A year before the actual discovery of

Ernest O. Lawrence
University of California, Lawrence Berkeley National Laboratory.

Element 94, Fermi was intending to find out if a chain reaction could be produced in natural, unseparated uranium. If that turned out to be possible, he suspected that U-238 could be induced to absorb neutrons to begin creation of the Element 94 predicted by Bohr and Wheeler.

The work at Columbia drew two scientists, Fermi and Leo Szilard, who apparently had independently thought of the possibility of creating a chain reaction in natural uranium. They were probably the two most talented scientists who could have collaborated for this work. They had high regard for each other's abilities, but they were an odd pair who had trouble working together.

Fermi was the rare combination of a theoretical physicist who worked out problems in his head but who was also willing and eager to devise and perform experiments to test his ideas. He was 38, fresh from winning a Nobel Prize a couple of years earlier.

Szilard was 42, the eccentric Hungarian refugee from Hitler's Europe who, in London in 1933, had been struck with the possibility of a nuclear chain reaction. He was a brilliant theoretical physicist, a constant source of ideas, most of them very good. (In fact, one scientist said that if success with the atom bomb depended on ideas alone, it would have taken only Leo Szilard.) But he disdained actually doing experiments, considering it "peasant work."

Fermi commuted to his Columbia lab from a suburban home in New Jersey where he lived with his wife and children. Szilard, who didn't marry until much later in life, preferred to live in a hotel near the university. He believed he did his best thinking in the bathtub in his hotel room. At the laboratory, he would explain what should be done to test an idea—and then stroll off down the hall, hands clasped behind his back, deep in thought. A young scientist working on the experiment recalled that Szilard "was not willing to do his share of the experimental work…He hired an assistant to do what we would have required of him." The hired assistant was competent. There was no complaint about that but it was not "Fermi's idea of how a joint experiment should be carried out."

The immediate question at Columbia was whether a pile of natural uranium could be arranged in such a way that the following would happen: An atom of U-235 fissions, emitting two or more neutrons. At least one of those neutrons splits another atom of U-235, which also releases two or more neutrons, and so on and so on. Would it keep the chain reaction going? And if that happened, would it be possible to control the chain reaction to prevent an almost instantaneous, destructive release of energy?

There were all kinds of complications to consider. As Fermi had discovered in Italy, U-235 atoms fission most efficiently when bombarded by slow neutrons, moving at a speed of "only" about 1.4 miles per second. But when an atom splits, it emits fast neutrons, moving at about 8,700 miles per second.

Somehow the scientists needed to manipulate the speed of neutrons. In Italy, Fermi had accidentally discovered that a wooden tabletop slowed neutrons, acting as a moderator, as did paraffin or water. The neutrons' loss of energy and speed was the result of collisions between neutrons and the nuclei of hydrogen atoms in water or paraffin. The nucleus of the hydrogen atom is one proton, about the same mass as a neutron. So if a neutron struck the proton, it would lose speed as it collided with the proton. In fact, the more equal in mass the neutron and the target particle, the greater will be the loss of energy (and speed) of the neutron. Think of it this way: If a speeding golf ball smacked into a bowling ball, the golf ball would bounce off with little loss of speed and have little effect on the bowling ball. But if two objects of equal size collide, such as croquet balls, the impact would slow the first ball considerably, and the lost energy would move the second ball.

Given that, it was obvious that the best moderator (or slower-downer, as Fermi called it) would be one of the lighter elements and one that did not absorb neutrons. Fermi and Szilard selected graphite, the common form of carbon (the sixth lightest element) largely because graphite appeared to be the most likely to be available quickly.

They began building a structure in which layers of natural uranium were separated by layers of graphite, the idea being that neutrons would collide with the nuclei of carbon atoms in the graphite and in bouncing around be slowed to the desired speed. It was almost like a cue ball banging into game balls and losing a little energy and speed with each collision. The layers—they called the arrangement a lattice—were a new idea. Previously, the thought had been to mix uranium and the moderator together. But painstaking measurements revealed that graphite in layers did a more predictable job of slowing the neutrons to the desired energy.

Fermi began calling the lattice structure a "pile." Years later, Segrè asked Fermi if he had adapted the word from another source of energy, the Voltaic Pile, the first electric battery invented in 1800 by another Italian, Alessandro Volta. To Segrè's surprise, Fermi said he hadn't even thought of Volta's pile, but meant the word only in the American sense, as in a heap of stuff. At any rate, the word "pile" stuck and is still used occasionally for nuclear reactors. The first pile went together at Columbia in the summer of 1941, a cube of graphite about 8 feet on a side with uranium oxide (the best grade of uranium they could get at the time) distributed through the graphite layers.

Success in producing a self-sustaining chain reaction depended on a crucial measurement, the multiplication factor k. Suppose there are 100 free neutrons in a pile. Some will be lost outside the pile, some will be lost to the graphite or impurities and some will be absorbed by U-238 without causing fission. But some will cause fission in U-235 atoms, releasing more neutrons. So if the original 100 neutrons caused fissions to produce, say, 105 new neutrons, k would equal 1.05 and the chain reaction would be self-sustaining. If only 99 new neutrons were produced, k would be 0.99 and the reaction could not sustain itself.

That's why the purity of both the uranium and graphite was so important to the pile builders—and in 1941 so daunting. Because of almost no commercial demand, the amount of purified uranium metal produced each year was only a few grams (there are 453 grams to a pound). Graphite was a problem as well, because no one had ever produced, or needed, graphite of the required purity. Procuring it was even more difficult because, with secrecy covering the project, they couldn't tell suppliers why they wanted it.

Fermi and Szilard's group built a couple of piles at Columbia, varying the design, attempting to improve the purity of uranium and graphite and constantly making measurements. Still, by the fall of 1941, Fermi told the federal Uranium Committee that k's best number so far was 0.87. There was hope, but no assurance, that higher quality uranium and graphite would increase the number.

Until 1941, America's investigation of possible atomic weapons had been on a relaxed, peacetime basis with work in laboratories scattered across the country. But by late in the year, the work had been centralized in a new agency armed with approval from President Roosevelt for an all-out effort to determine if atomic weapons were possible. There were several reasons for the change: 1) Element 94 presented a potentially quicker route to a bomb. 2) A memo from Great Britain, received in mid-summer, revealed that British scientists felt there was "a reasonable chance that an atomic [uranium] bomb would be produced by the end of the war." 3) There was good evidence the Germans were also experimenting with uranium.

A National Academy of Sciences committee studying the potential of an atomic bomb issued its third and most encouraging report late in November 1941. Echoing the cautious optimism of the British, it stated, "If all possible effort is spent, one might...expect fission bombs in significant quantity within three or four years." But it still referred only to uranium bombs with no mention of Element 94.

As secrecy enveloped the work, the old Uranium Committee had been code-named S-1 and was part of the new Office of Scientific Research and Development (OSRD). With new muscle from President Roosevelt's approval, the S-1 committee met in Washington, D.C., on December 6, 1941. The committee laid out assignments for developing uranium-bomb material and design of a weapon—but still no mention of Element 94.

After the meeting, three of the scientists went to lunch at the old Cosmos Club, a place with a prestigious history, that at the time was across Lafayette Square from the White House.

Arthur H. Compton, chairman of the National Academy committee and a member of S-1, suggested that the committee should give further thought to Element 94 as an alternative to the difficult separation of uranium-235.

Compton's luncheon companions were skeptical. Vannevar Bush, director of the OSRD, pointed out that the process was completely unknown to industry and that Fermi's primitive piles had not yet produced Element 94. James B. Conant, S-1 chairman, worried that, even if 94 could be produced in a chain reaction, learning how to separate it from the uranium could take years.

Vannevar Bush and Arthur H. Compton, 1940.
University of California, Lawrence Berkeley National Laboratory.

Compton replied: "Seaborg tells me that within six months from the time [94] is formed he can have it available for use in the bomb."

Conant, a professor of chemistry, retorted: "Glenn Seaborg is a very competent young chemist, but he isn't that good."

Despite doubts, Bush and Conant agreed that 94's possibilities should at least be investigated, and Compton accepted the responsibility. "Thus it was really as an afterthought...I was given authority to see what could be done toward developing [94]," Compton recalled. "Except for this afterthought, there might well have been no development of the nuclear reactor as a wartime project."

Later Seaborg said he had no memory of making such a confident prediction but added that as a young man ignorant of "the ultimate magnitude of the project," he probably had said something like it.

Note the date of the "afterthought" luncheon: December 6, 1941, the day before Japan attacked Pearl Harbor, bringing the United States into World War II. Those three names—Bush, Conant, Compton—may be little remembered now but are interesting examples of how scientists and their universities went to work for the nation.

Vannevar Bush (his first name was pronounced Van-EE-var; everyone called him Van) was 51, an engineer and president of the Carnegie Institute in Washington, D.C., a well-funded private institution that supported a variety of scientific projects. He had become increasingly unhappy with the lack of coordination between science and the government's early efforts to mobilize for possible war. And he must have been as good a talker as he was an engineer. In 1940 he had convinced President Roosevelt that the nation needed an agency that would coordinate science for national defense—and that he, Bush, was the man to head that office. He quickly moved the S-1 Committee into the OSRD so he could direct funding to needed work. In effect, he became what today we would call the nation's technology czar, while still president of the Carnegie Institute.

James B. Conant, September 1942. *University of California, Lawrence Berkeley National Laboratory.*

James B. Conant, 48, was president of Harvard University. Like Bush, he advocated closer coordination between science and the defense effort. As German troops overran France and the Low Countries in 1940, he had advocated direct aid to Great Britain, angering Harvard's students, most of whom favored strict neutrality. Bush recruited Conant as his deputy at OSRD and as S-1 chairman.

Arthur H. Compton, 49, was professor of physics at the University of Chicago and a Nobel laureate. He also worried that science was being neglected as war loomed.

None of these three went on the government payroll. The Carnegie Institute continued Bush's $25,000 salary even as he spent almost all his time on government work. Conant spent most of his time in Washington, once asking Harvard to reduce his $25,000 salary by 40 percent but the school agreed only to a 25 percent reduction. Compton's pay came from the University of Chicago.

Within months of the "afterthought" that began full-scale work on Element 94, Compton centralized the work at the University of Chicago. By early February 1942, he had established the Metallurgical Laboratory, a name selected to avoid attention and usually shortened to Met Lab. The university moved its mathematics department to make an entire building available to the Met Lab. The consolidation brought Fermi and Szilard and their chain-reaction research from Columbia University, Seaborg and his team from Cal's Radiation Lab, and selected scientists from other universities and industrial labs.

Met Lab had three goals and no one was sure if any one of them was actually attainable: 1. Produce a nuclear chain reaction. 2. Operate it at high enough power to create Element 94. 3. Learn how to separate 94 from uranium and then reduce it to metal, a form usable in a bomb. And do all this quickly enough for use in the war.

Finding money was no longer a persistent problem. With backing from President Roosevelt himself, the nation was committed to an all-out program.

A crew of machinists and millwrights built an amazing series of 30 different piles in the first months of 1942, each with alternating layers of graphite and uranium. Each pile was a little different—graphite bricks of different shapes and sizes, varying the distance between lumps of uranium. Machining graphite into bricks was dirty work.

Leona Marshall Libby
Department of Energy.

The workers remembered they looked like coal miners at the end of the day.

None of those piles achieved a chain reaction, nor were they expected to. Measurements from each succeeding pile revealed information for the design of a better and larger pile. Instruments were developed as they were needed to measure things that had never been measured before. Leona Woods (later Leona Marshall Libby), the youngest member of the group, built some of the neutron detectors that kept track of the multiplication factor k. She had been recruited by Fermi, almost by accident. Her son recalled that Miss Woods, a 23-year-old graduate student, had told one of Fermi's group that "You guys have discovered how the chain reaction works." Fermi apparently decided anyone that smart should be part of the effort. She was the only woman in the group.

The ninth of the intermediate piles at the Met Lab produced a k factor of 0.98, closer to the goal. For the first time as Fermi worked his slide rule, it appeared theoretically possible that a much larger pile could exceed the magic 1.0 k.

A sense of urgency permeated the project. Seaborg, who had arrived at the Met Lab in April, said most of the scientists were motivated "by the fear of what would happen if the Germans got there first." Most believed the Germans were as much as two years ahead. The war was not going well for the United States and its allies. Much of the Navy's Pacific Fleet had been destroyed at Pearl Harbor and Japan had overrun parts of Southeast Asia. German troops had conquered most of Europe and North Africa and were advancing deep into the Soviet Union.

"It's hard for anyone who didn't live through World War II to imagine the desperation and sense of impending doom that we felt," Seaborg remembered. Leona Woods recalled, "We were told day in and day out that it was our duty to catch up with the Germans."

Industry, helped along by nagging from the Met Lab, undoubtedly felt the same urgency as it developed better and quicker methods of producing high-quality uranium and graphite—all the while wondering at the sudden need for tons of it. Industrial scientists couldn't be let in on the secret project, of course, but if any of them had read newspaper science stories about splitting the atom, published before secrecy clamped down, they would have had a hint.

Finally in November 1942, with six tons of uranium metal on hand and a better grade of graphite that snatched 20 percent fewer neutrons than before, the Met Lab group began building a pile that, in theory, should go critical (achieve a chain reaction). Compton had taken over space for construction of the piles in a squash court under the west grandstand of the university's football stadium. (The university had discontinued football several years earlier.)

The secrecy of the project is hard to imagine today. Neither the university president nor the trustees were aware of the attempt to create the world's first nuclear chain reaction—on their campus, in a major city. Even Conant, S-1 chairman, didn't know of the plan at first. He turned pale when Compton told him, perhaps wondering what would happen if he'd tried it at Harvard. But by that time, the project was too far along to halt.

Actually, there would have been little possibility of the pile exploding like a bomb, but there was danger. If it turned out that a chain reaction couldn't be controlled, the rapid fissioning of U-235 atoms would release a great amount of heat, enough to cause an explosion that could blow the pile all over Chicago's South End. Superheated bits of uranium metal could have started fires for blocks around. Add to that, the debris would be highly radioactive.

With those possibilities in mind, the pile builders proceeded with great caution. Experience with the intermediate piles had told them how big the pile would need to be for criticality (that is, enough neutrons released to maintain a chain reaction). The working segment of the pile, the part with uranium embedded in graphite, was to be spherical because a sphere has less surface area than a cube—less area for neutrons to escape. Six tons of uranium metal, the best stuff, was distributed near the center of the lattice arrangement. More tons of less-pure uranium oxide lumps were placed farther from the core.

Theory said the pile would become critical when it reached a certain size, triggered by a neutron released when an atom fissioned spontaneously. To make sure that didn't happen unexpectedly, control rods containing boron or cadmium—notorious neutron eaters—were placed in slots through the pile. In place, they kept k well below 1.0. To increase the multiplication factor, the rods could be withdrawn, inch by inch.

Construction of the pile continued for 24 days with the number of liberated neutrons increasing with each layer of uranium and graphite; k kept within bounds by the control rods. Fermi with his slide rule had predicted almost the exact layer of graphite and uranium that would make the pile critical. But even Fermi was surprised when the pile approached criticality at only three-quarters of the height he'd calculated. So instead of the planned shape, the spherical working part of the pile turned out to be flattened on top. At that point, a chain reaction waited only for the control rods to be inched out of the pile.

From the outside, the pile looked like a black block about 20 feet high, topped by a dome where the core was flattened, the whole thing supported by a timber framework. Oh yes, one more striking feature: a huge rubberized cloth balloon was draped on three sides of the pile. It was a square balloon, maybe the only one ever made. Goodyear Tire & Rubber, more accustomed to making gasbags for blimps, must have wondered about the aerodynamics of a square balloon. Because of secrecy, they couldn't be told.

Early on, Compton had predicted a chain reaction would be possible if air were excluded from the reaction to avoid neutrons being stolen

Artist's rendering of the pile built at the University of Chicago in 1942.
Department of Energy.

An ancient chain reaction

Enrico Fermi's group was apparently one-upped by nature in achieving the first nuclear chain reaction—by about two billion years. Scientists working at the Oklo uranium mine in Gabon, West Africa, in the early 1970s found that uranium ore in several areas of the mine contained only about half as much of the isotope uranium-235 as elsewhere in the world. In fact, the ore samples resembled depleted uranium that has been run in modern power reactors. The answer: A set of special conditions had come together deep underground to trigger a series of chain reactions—conditions that apparently never happened again and never will.

Uranium-235 today comprises 0.7 of one percent of natural uranium. Figuring U-235's decay rate backwards, the isotope would have made up about 3 percent of natural ore two billion years ago, about the level to which uranium is enriched today for power reactors. The naturally rich uranium alone couldn't have gone critical, but thousands of feet underground there was pressure, heat, and—essential—ground water seeping into the ore. The water acted as a moderator to slow the neutrons ejected by fissioning U-235 atoms so they would be more likely to be absorbed by U-238 atoms, eventually resulting in small amounts of plutonium.

The heat of fission would soon turn the water to steam, removing the moderator and stopping fission. Scientists estimated the reactions would have lasted about 30 minutes before heat boiled off the water, stopping the reaction for about two and a half hours until the ore cooled and water entered again for another 30-minute run—about eight cycles a day over maybe a million years. They finally stopped for good when the U-235 component was depleted.

It couldn't happen again. Worldwide the proportion of fissionable uranium-235 in natural ore has decayed to where artificial enrichment is necessary to achieve a chain reaction. Oklo's deeply buried fission products have moved only about 10 feet in a billion years—a fact mentioned by the U.S. Department of Energy when discussing the safety of underground disposal of nuclear waste.

by the nitrogen in air. If necessary, they could have enclosed the pile in the balloon and pumped out most of the air. It did not turn out to be necessary; the pile was more eager to go critical than anticipated.

The big moment came a little after 3:30 p.m. on December 2, 1942. The group of scientists stood on a balcony above the squash court. Miss Woods, the graduate student, was recording measurements as they were called out. Fermi, slide rule in hand, called for the control rods to be pulled out, little by little. Neutron-counting instruments clicked faster and faster until the clicks became a blur, too fast for the ear to distinguish.

Fermi silently watched the instruments and then smiled. He closed his slide rule and said, "The reaction is self-sustaining."

The first chain reaction achieved by humans ran for 28 minutes until Fermi ordered the control rods inserted. The clicking slowed, a pen tracing the reaction on a roll of paper slid toward zero. Despite fierce activity within the core, the pile had worked in utter silence. Nothing moved, no lights flashed. The only sounds were from the instruments and voices calling numbers. The pile had operated at a power level of about one-half watt, enough to power a flashlight bulb. There was no provision to remove heat nor was there shielding against radioactivity. Presumably there would have been traces of Element 94 in the uranium after the pile sat for a few days.

The run had achieved a k factor of 1.0006, barely past the magic number. But it was a world-changing event even if few outside the squash court knew it had happened. It established beyond doubt that a self-sustaining chain reaction can be produced in natural uranium and—even more important—can be controlled.

There were mixed emotions. Eugene Wigner, a Hungarian scientist, had brought a bottle of wine and passed around paper cups, celebrating a major scientific achievement. Twenty-five years later Wigner wrote that he remembered feeling "the vague apprehensions of a man who has done something bigger than he ever expected to." Leona Woods remembered thinking, "Let's hope we are the first." Szilard solemnly shook Fermi's hand, saying he feared it would be remembered as a "black day in the history of mankind."

Abandoned White Bluffs Main Street in 1945, two years after the government took over the area for the Hanford plutonium development.
Department of Energy.

Chapter 6

Chain Reaction

T he question to the young chemist was direct and troubling: "Can you guarantee me a yield of 50 percent?" A lot was riding on the answer—success or failure of one of America's biggest wartime projects, perhaps the outcome of the war itself.

Crawford H. Greenewalt in 1945.
Hagley Museum and Library.

It was June 1, 1943. The questioner was Crawford H. Greenewalt, the 40-year-old engineer DuPont had assigned to work with scientists at the Met Lab at the University of Chicago. It was a tough question and pivotal to whether America would be able to make a plutonium bomb to use in World War II.

Six months earlier scientists at the Met Lab had achieved the first nuclear chain reaction, a tiny, necessary step toward the big reactors that would produce plutonium at Hanford. The challenge now was to figure out the best way to separate newly created Element 94, plutonium, from the uranium that had been bombarded with neutrons, a process that also created dangerously radioactive fission products.

Possibilities had been narrowed to two: A well tested procedure that worked but unfortunately produced such a corrosive mix that it tended to eat its way through anything containing it, or another method that theoretically shouldn't work at all, but unexplainably did.

Greenewalt, a brilliant chemical engineer who had helped DuPont develop nylon during the 1930s, put the question to Glenn Seaborg, 31, who two years before had discovered Element 94. Against the advice of older and more experienced chemists, Seaborg was favoring the method that defied theory.

In fact, it had been discovered more or less by accident. A search for ways to isolate 94 from a fiercely radioactive mix had begun while Seaborg was still at the University of California. It involved dissolving the whole nasty combination in acid and then experimenting with different chemicals, one after the other, to see if one could be found that would combine with 94 to form a solid that would precipitate out of the solution, leaving the nasty stuff behind. Nothing worked.

Finally one of the Met Lab scientists, nearing the "least likely" end of the list of possibilities, tried adding bismuth phosphate to the solution. It didn't work either. But the experimenter, Stan Thompson, whom Seaborg had "rescued" from a boring job at Standard Oil, followed a hunch and tried a significantly higher concentration of the same chemical. Surprisingly, it combined with Element 94 so well that the bismuth-phosphate method became one of the two candidates.

There was strong opposition within Met Lab to the puzzling method. Seaborg remembered that James Franck, head of the chemistry division and Nobel laureate, insisted it would be irresponsible to adopt a technique they didn't understand. The laboratory process using quantities that wouldn't even fill a test tube would need to be scaled up a billion times to make enough 94 for a bomb, a scale-up never attempted before. And would use a technique that shouldn't work.

Seaborg agonized over the decision: "How could I be sure?" he wrote later. "How could I oppose a man of Franck's reputation?... What if the Germans beat us to the bomb because we'd picked the wrong process?...The entire war might turn on this question."

But when Greenewalt asked if Seaborg could guarantee a yield of 50 percent, a poor yield that would have wasted half the Element 94, Seaborg was certain he could do at least that well. Without hesitation he answered, "Yes."

Within days, Greenewalt approved the controversial bismuth-phosphate process and DuPont's engineers began to design buildings to house the unexplained process, the mammoth plants that would rise at Hanford. Conventional chemical plants were old stuff to DuPont's engineers but this involved processes no one had ever done before. What they had to work with was a flow chart describing how Seaborg's group changed the chemical characteristics of the locked-in plutonium atoms in order to separate them from the uranium.

In greatly simplified terms, the mixture of uranium, plutonium, and fission products, after removal from the reactor, is dissolved in acid. A chemical, an oxidizing agent, added to the mix reacts with plutonium atoms to strip away four electrons. In this phase, missing four electrons, plutonium combines with bismuth phosphate to form a solid crystal. The solid precipitates from the solution, leaving behind unwanted debris. But the plutonium is still bound to the bismuth phosphate.

The solid crystal is then dissolved in another acid bath and an oxidizing agent is added again to strip two more electrons from the plutonium atoms. In this phase, with six electrons missing, plutonium no longer combines with bismuth phosphate, which precipitates out, leaving the plutonium behind, still in solution. Because the plutonium is not pure enough however, another chemical, a reducing agent, is added to the plutonium solution to restore two electrons to the plutonium atom. With the plutonium now missing four electrons, it will combine again with bismuth phosphate, precipitate out…and so on, over and over to achieve the purity needed. The process worked, although the chemists were not sure why. A final complication, which underscores the complex challenge facing the design engineers, is that the entire process had to be done behind heavy shielding and by remote control due to fierce radioactivity.

Even the engineers who had designed DuPont's nylon manufacturing plants during the 1930s had never seen anything like this. The company had taken almost ten years from the time one of its scientists discovered how to draw a molecule into a fiber to marketing the material for women's hose. Researchers had tried different chemical combinations, repeatedly refined the process, and even sent samples to a knitting mill to make sure laboratory techniques would work on a manufacturing scale. (The trial at the mill was so secret that the research chemist who delivered the samples slept with them on the train.)

But in mid-1943 the engineers didn't have ten years to learn how to separate plutonium on a production scale. Construction would soon begin on the first reactor at Hanford, which itself would be a massive scale-up from the tiny pile at Met Lab. In a little more than a year it would begin producing plutonium that would need to be separated from a mix of uranium and fission products.

DuPont built a small pilot operation to test the separation process—a reactor to bombard uranium with neutrons and a plant to separate plutonium from the resulting mix. The small operation went up in Tennessee where huge plants to separate the rare uranium-235, the other likely ammunition for an atomic bomb, were already under construction.

The small reactor in Tennessee achieved a chain reaction on November 4, 1943, and ran for six weeks before the first irradiated uranium was ready and the bismuth-phosphate separating method could be tested. Seaborg remembered that some chemists were still so sure it wouldn't work that "they were betting money against it right up to the moment the plant began to run." They lost their bets; the method immediately bested Greenewalt's requirement of 50 percent yield. Within a few months, with tweaking, the plutonium yield was between 80 and 90 percent. Still, for years it was not fully understood why the bismuth-phosphate technique worked at all.

The first plutonium produced and separated at the pilot plant in Tennessee arrived at the Met Lab on January 1, 1944. It was only about 1,000th of a gram. (It would take about 28,000 such shipments to make an ounce.) Still, it was almost as much plutonium as had been produced to that date in all laboratory-scale efforts. As more shipments arrived, Met Lab scientists were able to learn more of the strange new metal's characteristics. Tiny bits were also sent for study to a new laboratory in Los Alamos, New Mexico, where work was underway on bomb design, both for plutonium and uranium-235 weapons.

Even before DuPont's engineers had a chance to look at the flow chart describing the controversial bismuth-phosphate process, a different kind of problem arose at the Met Lab. As Fermi's group

Plutonium in a suitcase

In the spring of 1943 the Met Lab in Chicago had lent a tiny sample of laboratory-produced plutonium to the bomb designers at the Los Alamos lab. The 200-microgram sample, too small to be visible, represented almost all the Met Lab's supply and was desperately needed back in Chicago for more study.

Glenn T. Seaborg, discoverer of plutonium, happened to be in Santa Fe and volunteered to take the sample on his return to Chicago. "The morning of our departure," Seaborg wrote, "the physicist Bob Wilson met us for a predawn breakfast to transfer the sample. For protection, he'd brought along his Winchester hunting rifle. The sample made the bus and train trip back to Chicago tucked in my suitcase."

was assembling uranium and graphite with growing confidence they would achieve a chain reaction, they were dismayed to learn that the Army was bringing in industrial help to design and build the massive reactors that would rise at Hanford. To them, it was a slap in the face. They felt it was their project and they should see it through to completion.

There were several factors at work. The European-educated scientists—Fermi, Wigner, Szilard, and others—had an inbred, almost cultural, distrust of industry. Even among the Americans, many of the younger men had never worked outside of university laboratories. And, frankly, few of them apparently realized the magnitude of the project. The tiny pile at the Met Lab, operating at a power of one-half watt, would be scaled up to the 250 million watts planned for Hanford's first production reactor. Producing plutonium for war was changing from science to engineering. Yet the scientists naively felt they should, and could, handle the whole job.

Arthur Compton, Met Lab director, described it as a "near rebellion" when he suggested the project would move faster with the help of a large industry already familiar with large-scale manufacturing. A protest meeting in June 1942 resulted in an impasse. Compton finally said those who would not accept industrial help were free to leave the project. None did, but the unhappiness lingered.

By the time of the protest meeting, the project was already moving out of the scientists' direct control. By June 1942, the Army Corps of Engineers had assumed responsibility for construction of the atomic-bomb plants. Brig. Gen. Leslie R. Groves was assigned in September to head the Manhattan Engineer District, which included work on both plutonium and uranium-235. By December 2, when Fermi's group achieved the chain reaction at the Met Lab, Groves had contracted with the DuPont Company to design and build the reactors and separation plants at Hanford.

Groves's first visit to Met Lab in October 1942 didn't make the scientists any happier. In fact, it was a near disaster. Already unhappy about the Army taking over the atomic-bomb project, the Met Lab scientists were prepared to dislike the hard-driving Groves—and they did. He apparently did not go out of his way to be charming. A chemist proudly invited Groves to view a precious sample of plutonium under a microscope. Groves gruffly said "I don't see anything…I'll be interested when you can show me a few pounds of the stuff."

It didn't help when one of the scientists, writing an explanation on a blackboard, made a mistake copying a figure from one line to the next. Groves, assuming he was being set up as an ignoramus, pointed out the mistake.

Groves, undoubtedly irritated, said, "You may know that I don't have a Ph.D.…But let me tell you that I had ten years of formal education after I entered college [apparently combining his time at universities and the Military Academy]. Ten years in which I just studied. I didn't have to make a living or give time for teaching. I just studied. That would be about equivalent to two Ph.D.s, wouldn't it?"

Seaborg, writing years later of that disastrous day, said Groves's behavior was typical, that he "was almost consciously abrasive, in stark contrast to the collegial tone we [scientists] were accustomed to." The impression Groves left at Met Lab that day was that the Army commander was arrogant and poorly educated.

Despite Groves's high opinion of his own abilities—and his willingness to mention it—those who knew him best and longest realized that despite his arrogance and unpleasantness, he was capable of understanding the essentials of highly technical problems and of successfully managing the biggest engineering project in the nation's history. Seaborg wrote that the way Groves ran the Manhattan Project "was nothing short of spectacular, with all the parts, including huge industrial projects, up and running successfully in time to go on to the next step that depended on them."

One long-time acquaintance said Groves was "the only person I have known who was every bit as good as he thought he was."

Groves often relied on his second in command, Lt. Col. Kenneth D. Nichols, to deal with the Met Lab scientists. "I knew the Chicago scientists liked Nichols better than they did me," Groves said later, "so I had him do most of the routine dealings with Compton and his people...If there was anything particularly touchy, I always had Nichols do it."

Col. Kenneth D. Nichols, second in command of the Manhattan Project, in 1945. *U.S. Army.*

Nichols had known Groves since the 1930s when both saw duty in Nicaragua, and there was no love lost between the two. Nichols had been assigned to the atomic-bomb project a few weeks before Groves came aboard as his boss and established headquarters in Washington. "I did not relish being under his direct control by being in the same office," Nichols wrote. "Consequently, in early October I arranged for orders transferring my permanent station to New York City." But the hard-charging, sometimes bullying Groves and the mild-mannered Nichols managed to work together for the duration of the atomic-bomb project.

Nichols, 34, looked scholarly, and he was. He had graduated at the top of his class from West Point, had studied in Germany, and had earned a doctorate in hydraulic mechanics at Iowa State University.

Nichols made a good impression at the Met Lab. On his first visit in the summer of 1942, he told Compton, "If you expect me to do my end of the job, you have to start educating me." The result, Nichols remembered, was that on later visits "Fermi or other scientists would give me an informal lesson. They all recognized my desire to learn and were eager to teach me what I needed to know." The doctorate, of course, added prestige at the Met Lab despite his Army uniform.

It wasn't long before Nichols was drawn into the protests against DuPont. At Compton's request, Nichols listened to the scientists complain that DuPont engineers were too conservative, too slow to make design decisions, and carried safety requirements to a "ridiculous point."

Nichols wrote later: "Finally, Enrico Fermi, in all seriousness, strongly recommended to me that we eliminate DuPont from all work except that of the chemical separation plant...He claimed that the Met Lab could design the reactors in half the time DuPont was taking and concluded, 'If you people will just hire for me the laborers and supply them with [graphite] brick, I'll tell them where to lay them.' Needless to say, I was surprised to hear such a claim coming from a man of Fermi's stature."

Although DuPont depended on the Met Lab for the research and design ideas, the company insisted on full responsibility for final design of the reactors and separation plants planned for Hanford. In a way, it reduced the scientists to blueprint checkers. Designs prepared in Wilmington, Delaware, at DuPont headquarters, were sent to Met Lab for checking and approval. Nichols recalled that the scientists continued to resent this secondary role.

The project was moving ahead with a speed and a secrecy that would be stunning today. The costs were hidden, more or less, in the Corps of Engineers' already huge budget. People anywhere near Hanford knew something big was going on but few had any idea what. One of the more popular rumors was that DuPont was building a plant to make nylon stockings.

A crucial mistake

A German scientist made a crucial mistake in January 1941, a time when Germany seemed to have a head start in research aimed at an atomic bomb. The error, a mismeasurement, seriously slowed work on one of the most promising routes to a weapon, adding to German scientists' doubts that an atomic weapon could be available in time for use in the war.

The mistake by Walther Bothe in early 1941 would have seemed unlikely. He was 50, a brilliant experimenter, and former director of the physics institute at the University of Heidelberg.

Scientific information had still flowed freely among nations in the 1930s and the Germans knew of the predicted—but still undiscovered—Element 94. Bothe was evaluating graphite as a possible moderator to slow down neutrons, a step toward production of Element 94 in a reactor fueled by natural uranium.

Bothe's measurements, using the highest quality graphite he could find, seemed to show that graphite would absorb too many neutrons to sustain a chain reaction. That left scarce, expensive heavy water as the Germans' only feasible moderator. Germany had a source of heavy water from a plant in Nazi-occupied Norway, but bombing by the British and sabotage by Norwegian resistance fighters severely limited the amount of heavy water reaching Germany, crippling reactor-building efforts. Heavy water is regular water enriched with deuterium (an isotope of hydrogen). Deuterium's nucleus contains a neutron in addition to a proton, doubling its mass. This greater density makes it a better moderator than normal water. In America, scientists considered using heavy water before deciding on graphite.

Bothe's mistaken measurement probably was caused by contaminants in the graphite. By this time, British and American scientists had begun withholding results of their nuclear work. Germany never made a concerted effort to gather nuclear scientists into centers to work together and share results, as happened in America, so Bothe didn't check his results against work elsewhere. As a result, largely due to Bothe's error, Germany gave up on widely available graphite, the moderator used in American labs.

There were other factors that worked against a German bomb. The government was more interested in research on weapons with immediate payoff—jet fighter planes, the V-2 rockets used against London—and diverted resources and scientific talent to those projects.

German scientists evaluated the other route to a bomb, using enriched uranium. They concluded it would be so time consuming and expensive there was little chance of such a weapon becoming available during the war.

After the war, some scientists maintained their interest in nuclear energy was for power production and they were never enthusiastic about an atomic weapon. Whatever the other reasons, Bothe's famous mistake effectively stopped German work on the most promising route to an atomic weapon.

The result? Hitler's Germany was never close to building an atomic bomb.

But wartime secrecy worked both ways; the U.S. Army and American scientists still considered themselves in a race with Germany. In late 1943, Gen. George Marshall, Army chief of staff, suggested that the Manhattan Engineer District form a special intelligence unit to follow advancing troops in Europe to search for information about German work on a bomb.

Brig. Gen. Leslie R. Groves selected scientific members of the team. The secrecy-obsessed general was briefly upset at the name chosen for the group, Alsos, which in Greek can mean "grove." He worried its similarity to his name might provide a clue to the project.

As the Alsos team followed Allied troops into Italy and then France and Germany, examining laboratories and questioning captured scientists, it became more and more obvious the Germans were not making a serious effort to build a bomb.

Finally, only weeks before Germany surrendered, the Alsos team found 1,100 tons of uranium stored in a salt mine in Germany. That prompted an April 23, 1945, memo from Groves to Marshall: "The capture of this material, which was the bulk of uranium supplies available in Europe, would seem to remove definitely any possibility of the Germans making any use of an atomic bomb in this war."

The race with Germany, never really a race, was over.

Wartime housing at Hanford, 1944.
Department of Energy.

Chapter 7

Continuing Secrecy

T he visitor showed up in Richland unannounced on December 7, 1943. He said he had been sent to investigate the secret Hanford project and wanted to talk to the Army officer in charge.

Fred A. Canfil told Lt. Col. Franklin T. Matthias that he was an investigator for the Truman Committee and was looking into complaints about the huge amount of land being acquired for the project. Canfil, 59, said he had been assigned by Harry S. Truman himself, the senator from Missouri and chairman of the committee.

Matthias and other top officials at Hanford knew that complaints from evicted farmers and landowners had reached Washington, D.C. In fact, Truman's committee, already making a name for itself exposing waste in war work, had written to the DuPont Company and the War Department during the summer asking for information on estimated costs, why Hanford had been chosen, and why so much land was needed. It had fallen to Secretary of War Henry Stimson to talk to Truman.

Stimson, 75, a man of tremendous national prestige, had previously served as secretary of state and secretary of war. In 1940 President Franklin D. Roosevelt asked him to return to service as secretary of war. So on June 17, 1943, when Stimson told Truman of Hanford's importance to the war effort and need for secrecy, Truman respectfully agreed to call off his committee. (Truman didn't learn what was actually going on at Hanford until he became president after FDR's death.)

Coincidentally, complaints of evicted Hanford landowners and concern over agricultural land being taken out of production came up at the president's cabinet meeting that same day, June 17, 1943, and FDR asked if the Hanford plants couldn't be built somewhere else. Again it was Stimson who convinced the president that Hanford best fit the project's needs for isolation, abundant water, and electrical power.

Matthias's diary entry for December 7, 1943, said he told Canfil of the agreement between Stimson and Truman and "that I could not permit him to do any work without checking with my headquarters." It was late in the day and Matthias noted, "I suggested he call Senator Truman in the morning to confirm his instructions, to which he agreed."

Canfil was described by acquaintances as "a character...very loud and blustery...most people were a little afraid of him." Matthias apparently kept the situation low key. In an interview some 40 years later, he remembered,

Fred A. Canfil attempted to investigate the Hanford project in 1943. *Sammy Feeback, Harry S. Truman Library.*

"I called [Gen.] Groves who called Truman who took action real fast."

It's not clear why Canfil showed up at Hanford six months after Truman had agreed to call off the investigation. Matthias thought Canfil probably was acting on his own "to earn Brownie points" with Truman. At any rate, neither Canfil nor the Truman Committee tried again. Canfil is remembered mostly as the man who gave Truman the desk sign, "The Buck Stops Here."

Congressman Compton I. White was refused entry to the Hanford site in 1944. *Public domain.*

Almost everyone in the Pacific Northwest knew that something big was going on at Hanford. A few months after Canfil's attempt, Congressman Compton I. White, of Idaho's First District, showed up unannounced at the project's Yakima Gate, the one used by workers commuting from the Yakima area. He said he wanted to look at the land being condemned. He was held and questioned for four hours under bright lights in a windowless

There had been a few newspaper reports that the Truman Committee would probe Hanford. Canfil's unsuccessful visit apparently started a rumor in nearby Pasco. Olav Skartland, my best friend since third grade, was home on leave from Navy flight training a few weeks after Canfil's attempted investigation. He remembers hearing this story from railroad workers: *"A special car arrived in Pasco on Northern Pacific Train No. 1 carrying Harry Truman and a team of investigators. They drove out to Richland and were turned away. Angered, they returned to Pasco and Truman phoned FDR who said, "Back off, Harry." They hooked up the car to No. 1 the next day and went on to Seattle."* Like many rumors, this one was seeded with a true event but grew to be wildly inaccurate. Olav was a little disappointed many years later when I told him what had really happened.

room, he claimed, getting angrier by the minute. The officer-of-the-day finally showed up and, because it was Sunday, escorted White to Matthias's house.

Matthias noted that he "talked to him for some time. He was very angry that he had been held up…He left feeling somewhat satisfied, I felt, although not entirely pacified." White, 66, a former railroader, logger, miner, and rancher, could have been a difficult customer to handle. But, as with Canfil, Matthias kept things calm. Groves told Matthias to write a letter of explanation to White but not to apologize.

Hanford's wartime power, reaching all the way to the White House, is almost unimaginable today. The project was funded by what is today called a black budget—maybe the nation's first—effectively invisible to probers. The project not only was untouchable to congressional investigators, but it repeatedly pulled rank on the Navy and the Army Air Corps.

The Naval Air Station near Pasco, commissioned July 31, 1942, was looking for an auxiliary landing field for use by flight cadets.

Army Air Corps officers at the new air base near Moses Lake wanted land near Hanford for a gunnery range. Matthias's diary entry for April 13, 1943, told how he dealt with both: "Air Corps and Navy officials in our area have been definitely told that our project cannot be disturbed and that our requirements have complete and absolute priority over theirs."

Capt. B.B. Smith, the first commanding officer of the Pasco Naval Air Station, was on the receiving end of some of the Hanford power. He remembered, presumably with some sarcasm, that, "when the Hanford project first started, Colonel Matthias came out to the Navy base stating that he had come to ascertain what our operations were and then determine whether he would close it down. By then we had been in operation a full year or more." As it turned out, Matthias did not object to continued operation of the Navy base. Smith's own Navy superiors turned down his request for a gunnery range at Priest Rapids near the Hanford project—and told him not to ask for reconsideration.

Hanford also shot down the Navy's plans for an auxiliary landing field at Vista in the Horse Heaven Hills area about five miles from Richland—well beyond the Hanford project boundary. "We'd arranged to purchase the land," Smith recalled, "had contracted to build…had stockpiled lumber at the site when suddenly the project was canceled and I did not know why." Six months later Matthias told him "we were sorry we had to cancel your plans."

Technically, Smith, a Navy captain, outranked Matthias, an Army lieutenant colonel. But as Smith recalled ruefully years later, "They could write their own ticket, and did!"

Keeping news about Hanford out of newspapers and off the radio proved to be tougher than keeping investigators out of the project. On June 28, 1943, the new Office of Censorship sent a Code of Wartime Practices to newspapers and broadcasters. It requested that nothing be published about a list of topics, actually mentioning atom splitting, atomic fission, radioactive materials, and new and exotic weapons. It also asked the media not to publish anything about nine elements;

uranium was mentioned but buried among others ending in -ium that had nothing to do with the wartime project.

The code went to 2,000 daily papers, 11,000 weeklies, and all the nation's radio stations. To the surprise of the censors and relief of the Army, the code was greeted with pretty much of a yawn. Many harried editors read it, probably wondering what the censors were trying to hide but not grasping its significance.

I assume a copy of the code arrived in the weekly *Pasco Herald*'s mail and the editor, my father, glanced over it and then filed it away. If he thought anything about it, he didn't mention it to our family. As far as I know, he didn't connect the topics mentioned in the code with Col. Matthias's visit four months earlier asking for secrecy—or with the huge construction job already underway at nearby Hanford.

For the most part, the nation's newspapers and broadcasters cooperated and there was no serious breach of essential information during the war. The few newspapers that had science writers in those years stopped reporting on nuclear research. American science journals stopped publishing results of nuclear research, a fact noted by German physicists who also were interested in the fission of uranium. Germans also noticed that several of the most prominent American scientists in the field had dropped out of sight, a pretty obvious clue that America was working on a secret atomic-weapons program.

The problem in the Pacific Northwest was that documents concerning land acquired by the Army and lawsuits by aggrieved landowners were filed in courthouses and editors justifiably felt it should be public information. At one point Matthias complained in his diary, "It is apparent that trying to restrict publicity on this project is like keeping water in a sieve."

In April 1944 the *Seattle Times* sought Army clearance to print a story describing the rushed construction of Richland Village to house DuPont scientists and administrators. It was an important story because the new village would quickly become one of eastern Washington's biggest cities. Richland was not behind barriers; anyone, enemy spies included, could see the activity. It's easy to imagine how difficult it was for the independent editors to seek the Army's

Henry MacLeod, *Seattle Times* city editor, in 1945.
Courtesy of the MacLeod family.

permission to publish a story. I doubt they would ask today.

Matthias objected to the proposed story. He noted that while the *Times* "article is not specifically objectionable in the material included, it is bad in that it emphasizes the speed and importance of the project." He called Henry MacLeod, city editor of the *Times*, who agreed to hold the story until they could talk. A few days later Matthias went to Seattle and explained the Army's objections. MacLeod agreed to hold the story but attached a condition: "He agreed [to keep] information out of print if I would give him my personal assurance that if the story of this project was announced from this area, that he would get the clearance as soon as any of the other newspapers in the area," Matthias noted.

Matthias told MacLeod he would do his best but warned that he could not guarantee that a national newspaper or magazine would not get the story. Matthias had heard several months earlier that Walter Graebner, a well-known correspondent for *Life* magazine, had talked to newspapermen in Spokane and Seattle, asking that they keep their eyes on Hanford and pass on as much information as possible. Matthias had relayed that tidbit to Groves "for such action as can be taken." *Life* did not use any significant news about Hanford until the bomb dropped on Japan. The *Seattle Times* did not use the Richland Village story until restrictions eased a bit later.

Disputes grew testier later in 1944 when the *Seattle Times* printed a story, without Army clearance, concerning lawsuits filed by landowners forced off their land. These were among the first to get the shocking order to leave their homes and among the first to accept settlements. But with better appraisals, later settlements were more generous and these lawsuits sought adjustments. The *Times* story, based on court records open to the public, was to be the first in a series of three.

The story apparently worried the Army, not so much for security but that publicity would encourage more lawsuits and cause more expense and delay in final settlements. Matthias dispatched Lt. Milton R. Cydell to talk to MacLeod, who agreed to hold the remaining two stories until Cydell could review them.

The next day Matthias talked to an angry Russell L. McGrath, *Times* managing editor, who pointed out that everything in the articles was public information and there was no rational reason it needed to be cleared with anyone. The conversation undoubtedly heated up. Matthias's diary simply said McGrath "took objection" to Matthias's claim that the *Times* had failed to keep its earlier agreement to get clearance on stories about Hanford. But, Matthias noted, McGrath finally "agreed that Lt Cydell and his people would go over future installments and eliminate all objectionable features."

Giving in would have been hard on McGrath, a stern, disciplined man who had always fought attempts to influence news coverage whether the attempts came from inside or outside the *Times*. It didn't help that Cydell was a former *Times* reporter and now, as a brand new Army lieutenant, was giving orders to his old boss. Looking back over more than half a century, McGrath was right. The information was public and the Army's objections had less to do with security than expediency. In normal times the newspaper would have been justified in running that story over the Army's objections. But they were not normal times and pressure from the Army and the Office of Censorship was strong, the war had wide public support, and everyone, including McGrath, wanted to do what they could.

Most of the newspaper and radio reports that worried the Army were unintentional, caused by ignorance of or misinterpretation of the censorship code. A few, however, were close enough to the facts to alarm the Army.

A report on the Mutual Broadcasting System on April 15, 1944, mentioned a project that would split the atom and create new weapons

Robley Johnson, chief photographer during construction of the Hanford plants, was cleared to see all aspects of the vast project. Still, the atmosphere of extreme secrecy occasionally surprised him.

"I remember making a picture one day and the next day I couldn't see it without a special pass," Johnson told me. "I'd printed and delivered it the day before and now I couldn't see it. And every time I turned around someone would see the camera and grab me. Sometimes they'd hold me up for an hour until they found out by telephone who I was. I used to have a real short temper—still do, I guess—and getting grabbed didn't help."

Despite access to the plants, he had no idea what they were for. Johnson operated a photo studio in Richland for many years after the war.

and said the work was near Pasco, Washington. An investigation revealed that the people who prepared the script had not checked the code and the announcer didn't know about the code. The Army asked the network to destroy all copies of the broadcast.

Drew Pearson, an investigative broadcaster and journalist who wrote the Washington Merry-Go-Round column for the *Washington Post*, had argued with the Office of Censorship about its Code of Wartime Practice early in the war and for a time had been required to get previous clearance for his radio programs. When he actually obtained accurate information about the atomic-bomb program in mid-1944, however, he cooperated and kept the secret until the bomb fell on Hiroshima.

An article in the *Lewiston (Idaho) Morning Tribune* on April 7, 1943, contained "facts concerning the [Hanford] project which are too accurate to be based entirely on rumor," Matthias noted. He asked Paul Nissen to check into it. Nissen, a civilian employee of the Army, had the thankless—and seemingly hopeless—job of convincing editors not to use stories about Hanford. Nissen found that the secretary of the Lewiston Chamber of Commerce had been in Pasco, talked to businessmen as part of his job, and then reported it at a meeting back home, again part of his job. Nissen suggested to Matthias the Army keep track of "visitors who might induce publicity" and warn them "to work on their home-town paper to prevent their publishing any of the information that might be brought back"—obviously an impractical solution. I never met Nissen, who must have shared Matthias's frustration with trying to bottle up news, but a few months later when I joined the Navy he rented what had been my room in the Williams family home in Pasco.

There were some odd leaks of information. A Mr. Scott of the *Spokane Chronicle* called Matthias on May 20, 1943, to ask about using a report from the *Chronicle*'s correspondent in Washington, D.C., that the Army was buying tons of silver to use at Hanford and Oak Ridge. The report apparently leaked from a closed session of the Senate Appropriations Committee. Matthias asked the *Chronicle* not to use the story and immediately phoned Groves. The story was hushed up but it was more or less true. The Army actually borrowed 14,700 tons of silver from the U.S. Treasury to use at Oak Ridge for windings on electromagnets under construction. Copper would have been preferred for the Oak Ridge project but was in extremely short supply in wartime and silver is about as good a conductor as copper.

Col. Kenneth D. Nichols, Groves's deputy, remembered signing an inventory "stating that we had in our possession over 400 million troy ounces of silver." The Treasury agreed to keep the transfer of metal secret and even continued to carry the 400 million troy ounces on its balance sheets. When the silver was returned to the Treasury after the war, despite having been melted and remelted and formed into windings and other parts for the magnets, only 0.036 of one percent of the 14,700 tons was missing.

Politicians in the Pacific Northwest were understandably frustrated at not knowing what was happening at Hanford. Their loose talk was usually harmless but still caught the attention of Army intelligence.

Matthias noted on April 29, 1944, a *Chicago Tribune* story reporting that Congressman Homer D. Angell of Oregon had told the U.S. House of Representatives that the Bonneville Power Administration was "building a secret project in the Northwest…part of the justification for [the BPA's] budget approval." The BPA administrator, Paul J. Raver, not only denied the story but also denied suggesting that Angell use it to support BPA's budget request.

The impact of the Hanford project on a relatively undeveloped central Washington, even while land was still being acquired, seemed astounding to those whose memories of the Great Depression were vivid. Kirby Billingsley, editor of the *Wenatchee World* and one of my father's cousins, wrote a friend in March 1943 that "The DuPont people and the Army have taken over 600,000 acres…people of White Bluffs, Hanford and other communities have 30 days to evacuate." (The first land acquisition actually amounted to about 430,000 acres.)

Karl Stoffel, secretary to Congressman Walt Horan, wrote back that the Army's contract with DuPont was so big and so secret that it went from the President to Gen. Marshall and on down without information on what the project was. Stoffel added that the contract was for "no ordinary defense plant or powder plant."

Obviously, neither Billingsley nor Stoffel knew the purpose of the Hanford project and probably didn't until the end of the war. What they knew, and wrote, was harmless as far as Hanford security, but the letters would have alarmed Matthias if he had known about them. Their comments were typical of astounded reactions all over the Northwest as the realization spread that the Hanford project was bigger than anything seen before—and was on fast forward.

Sometimes the information leaks came from contractors building the Hanford plants. Army intelligence in San Francisco telephoned Matthias on April 15, 1944, that Morrison-Knudsen's annual report mailed to stockholders included many classified "bits of information about our project," even some cost figures. Matthias noted that "efforts will be made to have the distribution of this report stopped and all copies returned." Morrison-Knudsen's contract was to build underground storage tanks that would hold highly radioactive waste from plutonium-separation operations.

Groves decided to handle this situation personally. It was a Saturday and he told Morrison-Knudsen he wanted to meet company principals "in Washington on Monday or in Chicago on Tuesday" for an explanation on why the information was published and what would be done to avoid repeating the lapse. It must have been humiliating for the company officials as the general raked them over the coals, not only for the security lapse but also for quality problems and delays on the underground waste-storage tanks. The company had complained previously that quality testing on the tanks was too rigorous.

Matthias later noted that Morrison-Knudsen had signed agreements acknowledging that its work at Hanford was covered by security codes and the Espionage Act. He added that a Mr. Olsen, a company official, "apparently feels that General Groves was unjust and unduly harsh in connection with both the security aspect…and in connection with the status of the job on the tanks."

Air space over the Hanford project was closed to all but the project's light planes flown by security personnel. Commercial airline routes, particularly Spokane to Portland, had to detour around the big project. The most frequent "intruders" were confused or lost Navy cadets flying the slow, old Yellow Peril primary training planes—open cockpit, biplane, fixed landing gear, 100 mph cruising speed—out of the Pasco Naval Air Station. The intrusions occasioned calls to the long-suffering Capt. B.B. Smith.

There was a more interesting violation of air space at 9:00 a.m. on September 7, 1943. A four-engine bomber flew so low over the river adjoining the project that it cut a telephone cable. Six days later Matthias heard from the Second Air Force Western Air Command that the offending pilot "has been identified and disciplinary action taken. Inasmuch as the pilot had overseas duty orders and left within a few hours after they discovered he was the culprit, the disciplinary action was not severe."

There was at least one effort to stifle sensitive information that had been available to the public for more than a year. William L. Laurence of the *New York Times* had written a long and detailed story about the Niels Bohr–John Wheeler theory that uranium-235 fissioned when bombarded with slow neutrons and that a chain reaction might be possible. (This was before plutonium was discovered.) The story, appearing May 5, 1940, had pointed out applications for both industry and military. It also reported that the Nazi government had assigned top German physicists to work on uranium fission.

Laurence hoped his story would spur government interest in nuclear work, still uncoordinated and underfunded in 1940. Instead, "nothing happened," Laurence recalled. He tried again, submitting a slightly revised version to the *Saturday Evening Post*. That article ran on September 7, 1940. He joked later that at the least "I expected to be called to Washington...for further details about such an important subject." Again, nothing happened.

When the government finally did get interested in nuclear chain reactions, it asked libraries to take the *Saturday Evening Post* article out of circulation and report the names of persons seeking copies. (Groves said later no requests were reported.) Laurence believed it was the last article in any American publication, scientific or popular, that mentioned atomic energy until the war ended. American investigators found a copy of the article in a German laboratory as the war in Europe ended. It had been clipped from the magazine, pasted in a scrapbook, and was accompanied by a complete translation into German.

Part Three

The Engineering

*…about 18 hours after startup the reactor died, shut itself
down. You can imagine the shock in the control room.*
September 20, 1944

The B Reactor.
Department of Energy.

The front face of B Reactor where workers loaded uranium slugs into 2,004 tubes. The reactor shut down in 1968. Today the area is set up for public tours.
Department of Energy.

Chapter 8

B Reactor

H anford's first reactor went critical a few minutes past midnight on Wednesday, September 20, 1944. It was less than two years since Enrico Fermi's team achieved the world's first chain reaction in Chicago, five years since Meitner and Frisch realized the "indestructible" atom could split, and 12 years since Chadwick discovered the neutron.

There was a festive atmosphere in the control room among the men—and one woman—who had guided construction of Hanford's B Reactor. Leona Marshall Libby recalled some of those "who had worked so hard for so many months" smelled "pleasantly of a drink or two of good whiskey."

As control rods were inched out and the reaction gathered strength, there must have been a strong sense of satisfaction among the scientists and engineers who had left their homes, their laboratories, sometimes their families, to work on a new weapon they hoped would end the war. Here it seemed that all the studies, experiments, long hours, and hard work were coming together successfully.

The big reactor, a prodigious scale-up from the half-watt power of the first pile in Chicago to a designed 250 million watts, worked in utter silence as neutrons zipped and collided at speeds of thousands of miles a second behind the massive shielding. Workers could hear the rush of river water pumped through the reactor to carry off excess heat, at a rate of 35,000 gallons a minute, going in at 50 degrees Fahrenheit and coming out at 140 degrees as planned.

Enrico Fermi had personally supervised loading the uranium fuel in B Reactor. (There was no A Reactor.) He was there that night as B Reactor started up, checking instruments and working his slide rule. So was Crawford Greenewalt, DuPont's head man on the plutonium project, who had witnessed the first chain reaction in Chicago.

B Reactor's power climbed to 9 million watts (far less than full power of 250 million watts) and held there as operators checked their instruments. Then, Libby remembered, operators began whispering to bosses and pulling control rods out a little, and then a little more. The reaction was inexplicably losing power. The operators kept pulling control rods farther and farther out as they tried to maintain power.

John A. Wheeler, the Princeton University physicist who had joined the DuPont team for the plutonium project, described B Reactor's unexpected behavior this way: "It was as if the engine of your car got sick as you were driving along a level road, and you had to push farther and farther down on the accelerator pedal to maintain speed; eventually, the pedal would be all the way to the floor and the car would start to slow down."

That's the way it was at B Reactor. Even with the control rods all the way out, power continued dropping during the day. By 6:30 p.m., about 18 hours after startup, the reactor died, shut itself down. You can imagine the shock in the control room. Walter O. Simon, Hanford plant manager for DuPont, recalled, "the silence was deafening…it was complete consternation."

Lt. Col. Franklin T. Matthias said, "It was a tremendous blow because we couldn't imagine that would happen."

For more than a year the Hanford project, with its gold-plated AAA priority, had pulled workers and materials away from other war projects, had consumed many millions of dollars, and had forced hundreds of people from their homes and farms. And now an essential part of the project, the reactor to produce plutonium for bombs, wouldn't work? Hanford, the white elephant of the 20th century? Endless congressional hearings? Such thoughts were probably swirling in the minds of Matthias, the DuPont people, and the scientists.

Fermi wondered if water was leaking from cooling tubes. That afternoon, workers circulated hot helium gas through the graphite moderator to flush out any possible leaked water. None was found.

Then, amazingly, B Reactor began to recover. By 1:00 a.m. the next day, it was operating steadily at low power. That afternoon operators pulled out the control rods until power again climbed to 9 million watts. And, as before, the reactor began shutting down.

The pattern of B Reactor's behavior—start up, climb to about 9 million watts, shut down, "rest" for about 11 hours, and then climb again to about 9 million watts only to shut down again—convinced Wheeler the reactor was poisoning itself. He reasoned the poison must be a fission product, created as the reactor gained power, with an enormous appetite for neutrons that was stealing enough of them to shut down the reaction.

Further, Wheeler reasoned, the poison must have a short half-life, decaying after about 11 hours to a point where the reaction could start up again. He checked a list of isotopes expected to be produced in fission and "looked for one with a half life somewhat less than, but not much less then, 11 hours." The reactor would need a little more time to start up than the actual half-life of whatever was poisoning it. Wheeler continued, "Immediately, xenon 135, with a half life of 9.2 hours, jumped out at me as the likely poison...There was no other candidate that readily accounted for the reactor's behavior."

Xenon-135 turned out to be the "daughter" of another fission product, iodine-135, which had an even shorter half-life. Iodine-135 was created as the reactor gained power but had decayed into xenon-135 by the time the reactor reached 9 million watts.

Embarrassingly, scientists had missed the poison at a smaller pilot reactor in Tennessee, which ran at much lower power. Wheeler had been aware of the possibility but had said self-poisoning should not be a problem if fission products had a cross-section for absorbing neutrons of no more than about 100,000 barns. (Fermi had come up with "barn" as a unit in measuring a target's ability to absorb neutrons, perhaps borrowing American slang for throwing at a barn door. The bigger the "barn," the more likely a neutron will hit a target and be absorbed.) Wheeler and everyone else were surprised that B Reactor would produce a fission product that could gobble enough neutrons to shut down the reaction.

In fact, it turned out that xenon-135 had a cross section 150 times greater than the most absorptive material then known, the cadmium used in control rods. It was as though the reactor itself had inserted control rods.

Except for some conservative engineering by DuPont, done over the objections of the Met Lab scientists, the startup failure of B Reactor would have been a disaster. There would have been two bad choices: Run B Reactor at low power in a stop-and-go mode that would take forever to produce plutonium, or start almost from scratch to design and build a new reactor to overcome the self-poisoning. Either way would have caused major delay, likely meaning a plutonium bomb would not have been available in World War II.

B reactor had been designed by a Met Lab team headed by Eugene Wigner, a refugee from Hungary. It was an efficient design that contained the precise amount of uranium to attain the planned power and produce plutonium—enough but no more, important because refined uranium metal was still in short supply. The working part of the reactor, 1,504 aluminum-lined tubes drilled completely through the graphite block, was in the shape of a cylinder lying on its side, about 36 feet high, 36 feet wide, and 28 feet deep. Uranium fuel—called slugs—would be pushed into the tubes. When the reactor was fully charged and the control rods pulled out, neutrons emitted by the fissionable U-235 in the uranium fuel would begin the reaction.

It was an elegant design—200 tons of uranium slugs filling tubes in the 1,200-ton block of graphite, the whole thing shielded inside a blocky building of steel and concrete.

The graphite block, of course, was in the shape of a cube and the cylindrical collection of tubes left the corners unused. The DuPont engineers looked at those corners and recommended that more tubes be drilled there, just in case they were needed. The Met Lab scientists, still resentful of the Army and DuPont taking over the project, objected vociferously to interference by the engineers.

Wheeler sided with the engineers. He had considered the possibility of poisoning but thought it remote, not imagining xenon-135's enormous appetite for neutrons. But he mentioned the possibility to the engineers. George Graves, Greenewalt's chief deputy, urged that the corners of the graphite block be drilled with 500 more tubes, just in case.

"Graves was guided in part by my advice," Wheeler wrote, "but perhaps even more by his industrial experience…and knew that a surprise or two was likely."

The scientists, incensed the engineers were questioning their judgment, continued to protest. DuPont asked the Army for backup. Col. Kenneth Nichols approved the extra tubes, remembering that "a good engineer always…adds a safety factor."

So 500 extra tubes had been drilled in the corners of the graphite block, making a total of 2,004 tubes. This extra work delayed completion of B Reactor and added millions to the cost, but the tubes were there when the reactor poisoned itself and died.

B Reactor museum?

With auxiliary buildings removed, B Reactor today stands alone. *Department of Energy.*

B Reactor was in operation for 24 years. It produced plutonium for the first atomic explosion in New Mexico in July 1945 and for the bomb dropped on Nagasaki on August 9, 1945. It continued production through much of the Cold War before being shut down permanently in 1968.

The B Reactor Museum Association, based in Richland, proposes the reactor be preserved and made available to the public as a "unique artifact of the beginning of the nuclear age," the first production reactor ever made. The National Park Service designated B Reactor as a National Historic Landmark in 2008.

Loading fuel into the still-empty tubes and connecting them to the cooling-water supply caused still more delay. When B Reactor finally reached full power three months after its shocking failure it was a "different animal" than it had been. Engineers had to learn by trial and error how to control it. Wheeler said it had two different modes of operation. Starting up, free of the xenon poison, the 2,004 tubes provided too much power and careful control was needed to keep it from getting out of hand. But at full power it needed the extra fuel to overcome the poison. Wheeler, good with similes, wrote that the big reactor "was like a race horse needing restraint as it eagerly waited to leap from the starting gate, but then needing goading to keep going after it had rounded the first curve and was tiring."

Even before B Reactor's stunning shutdown, another crisis had threatened to delay the project. As B Reactor neared completion— expected startup in September—concern mounted during the spring and summer that fuel slugs wouldn't be ready in time, and that the big, expensive reactor would stand idle.

Preparing the slugs was a complicated process beginning when refined uranium metal arrived at Hanford in the form of billets about four and a half inches in diameter and 12 to 20 inches long. Each weighed 250 to 325 pounds. (Uranium is heavier than lead and at this stage relatively safe to handle.) The billets were heated and extruded into rods and then cut into pieces about eight inches long and a little less than an inch and a half in diameter, each weighing about eight pounds. The slugs were then machined to precise size and turned on a lathe to the required diameter.

However, the scientists at Met Lab had decided the uranium slugs had to be encased in aluminum to keep fission products in and water out. It was this "canning" process that caused the trouble. The can had to be in complete contact with the slug inside so heat from fission could be transmitted to cooling water. No bubbles or gaps inside. The can had to be sealed as nearly perfect as possible. Water leaking into the can could cause the uranium slug to swell, distorting and possibly bursting the can and releasing dangerously

Hands up!

Leona Libby and Enrico Fermi decided one day to enjoy their sack lunches in the outdoors. It was Fermi's second day at Hanford and he wanted a look at the desert. They wandered past a guard office into the sagebrush and settled down with sandwiches. It wasn't long before a small airplane began circling overhead. Next they noticed a man with a pistol following their tracks in the sand. He told them to put their hands up. Libby remembered: "Fermi put up his sandwich and I put up my apple…We walked back carefully, with sandwich and apple held high…and identified ourselves at the gate." They finished their lunches inside.

radioactive fission products into the cooling water—and into the Columbia River.

The trouble was that the scientists who designed the can hadn't figured out how to actually do the job. Pressing a lid on the can crumpled the aluminum, the thickness of a few sheets of paper. As weeks went by, DuPont's Greenewalt finally decided that the Met Lab scientists, as scientists sometimes do, were amassing a lot of data but not showing much progress. So in March 1944, only months before the hoped-for startup of B Reactor, DuPont moved all canning work to Hanford.

The problem was finally solved by the people on the ground at Hanford, engineers and workmen who applied ingenuity and skills learned from other jobs to the first-ever task of making fuel for the largest nuclear pile ever assembled.

The first loading of B Reactor required 70,000 uranium slugs. Preparing reactor fuel has been improved and speeded up tremendously since World War II, but for the world's first production reactor it was a manual, one-by-one process.

Each core was dipped into molten metal three times during the processing. An operator using tongs would dip and swish each core in baths of bronze and tin, 45 seconds in each bath. Each core was then whirled in a centrifuge to fling off excess tin. The third bath, an aluminum-silicon alloy, provided a bonding agent between the core and the aluminum can and lid.

Finally, the tricky job of sealing the core inside the can without ruining the can was solved by the workers, an ingenious solution they called "underwater canning." The coated uranium core went into another bath of the molten aluminum-silicon alloy and, while still submerged, was fitted into the can and the lid put in place, all done by an operator using tongs.

The "underwater canning" was even more difficult because only a few degrees separated the melting points of the alloy bath and the can. The temperature in the canning furnace had to be precisely maintained to avoid melting the aluminum can. The can was encased in a steel jacket to maintain its shape and dimensions during the high-temperature canning.

Finally, the slug was quenched with cold water and the steel jacket removed. But there were still a dozen steps and inspections before the slug was ready to be sent off to B Reactor. The lid was welded on the can; even skilled welders had to learn new techniques for a job never done before. Each slug was tested for flaws by fluoroscope, pressure, and heat—with visual inspections of each core (all 70,000) after each step—before they were loaded on a railroad car and transported on newly laid tracks to B Reactor.

More than half the slugs were still failing inspections by mid-summer. By August 31, 1944, Matthias reported in his diary "a much higher percentage of slugs clearing the rigorous tests"—about 75 percent acceptable. The success rate continued to improve.

Despite the shock when B Reactor shut itself down shortly after its first startup, DuPont made the best of the resulting delay by running the reactor in stop-and-go mode at gradually increasing power levels

Emergency concerns

In 1944, with B Reactor nearing completion, DuPont headquarters in Wilmington, Delaware, was pressing for a practice evacuation in case of an emergency after the plants began operation. Matthias and Gen. Groves opposed it not only because of time lost but, as Matthias noted in his diary, it could be "disastrous to the project as it might cause a large number of people to leave if their fears for safety were increased."

After much dickering, DuPont and the Army compromised on a watered-down version of the original plan that would have moved everyone back to near Richland. Instead, on August 29 workers were evacuated from the B Reactor area in 13 minutes, but only to outside the fence surrounding the reactor. D Reactor, also under construction, achieved it in 18 minutes. Matthias noted that the drill "in general went off well...slightly over 5,000 men were evacuated."

DuPont continued to urge more realistic drills but apparently they were never conducted.

while the extra tubes were connected to cooling water and fuel loaded. During one of the shutdowns on November 6, partly "cooked" fuel slugs—totaling about six tons—were pushed out of 42 tubes. After cooling in water, they were moved to a separations building for use by workers learning how to handle the deadly material. Matthias noted that historic step with a laconic diary entry: "Run of hot material started."

B Reactor, with all 2,004 tubes loaded, finally reached and maintained full power (about 250 million watts) on December 28, three months after its shocking shutdown.

"Cooking" time for the uranium fuel, usually about 100 days, was critical. Fuel near the center of the reactor was subjected to a higher neutron flux and required less time. The physicists made calculations for each of the 2,004 tubes, based on time in the reactor and heat produced. When they figured some of the tubes were ready, workers would shut down the reactor and use high-pressure water to push the "cooked" slugs out the back of the reactor into a tank of water. Then fresh slugs would be loaded in the front side. Usually about 25 percent of the channels would be discharged during each shutdown, amounting to 60 or so tons of irradiated fuel.

Discharging was the most hazardous reactor work. Workers in elevators on both sides of the reactor removed the end caps from tubes, both front and back. Once done, the men on the discharge side would raise their elevator out of the way and retreat behind shielding as the irradiated slugs, lethally dangerous, were pushed out. The discharge crew used periscopes to monitor the slugs falling into a water tank where they stayed for a while to allow the more dangerous, short-lived fission products to decay away.

The next task, separating the plutonium, was daunting. The irradiated fuel contained about 250 parts plutonium per million parts of the nasty mix of uranium and fission products—ounces of "product" in a ton—a difficult and fiendishly dangerous activity. However, the chemical procedures for separation had been established, the huge separation buildings were nearing completion, and there was considerable confidence that retrieving those ounces of plutonium per ton would be possible.

Chapter 9

Consequences of Nuclear Reactions

W hen cooling water began running through Hanford's B Reactor in late 1944, it marked the first time humans had intentionally released large quantities of radioactive material directly into the environment. Water from the Columbia River ran through the operating reactor just once, cooled a few hours in an open basin, and then flowed back into the river.

A few weeks later, about 10 miles from B Reactor, the complicated process of extracting plutonium from irradiated fuel slugs began, sending great brown clouds containing radioactive contaminants out smokestacks. The discharges to the atmosphere were unfiltered, uncleansed. The only mitigation was extra air pumped into the stacks to dilute the gas, with the assumption it would be further diluted and dispersed by the wind.

Today such releases to river and air would be unacceptable, even unthinkable. But in 1944, there was relentless pressure to build an atomic bomb as quickly as possible in hopes it would end the war. President Franklin D. Roosevelt himself, the commander-in-chief, had approved an all-out effort. The pressure for speed as well as the newness of the technology led to safety measures that, if considered at all, were assumed to be temporary.

Admittedly, public attitudes were different in the 1940s. Many cities used rivers as sewers. Industries dumped untreated waste in rivers and lakes and sent toxic clouds of smoke toward the sky. Hanford was different in that the pollutant, radiation, was largely unfamiliar to the general public. Radiation's effects, whether harmful or useful, were only partly known even to scientists who had worked with it. And because of the project's secrecy, the discharges to river and atmosphere were without the usual public or government scrutiny.

Recognizing the unknowns, the Army Corps of Engineers began arranging some of the first studies of effects of radioactive pollutants more than a year before B Reactor started up.

In the summer of 1943, a 40-year-old assistant professor of fisheries at the University of Washington received what must have been a puzzling request: that he study the effects of radiation on fish, particularly salmon. He certainly knew about salmon but had never worked with radiation. He was told that the study related to the Columbia River

Lauren R. Donaldson began studying the effects of radiation on fish in 1943.
University of Washington Library Special Collections.

but secrecy required his work be done on campus. Neither he nor his employer, the university, was to know why he was doing it, except that it was of great importance to America's war effort.

A less determined man than Lauren R. Donaldson might have been intimidated at the assignment. Almost nothing was known about radiation effects on aquatic animals, including fish. Some research had been done on dry-land animals that had the advantage of remaining in one place. Donaldson's research would involve radiating salmon eggs or young fish and then having them disappear to sea for several years before they could be studied, and probably doing it for generation after generation of fish.

The aim was to learn what, if any, effects there would be on fish exposed to river water that had cooled a nuclear chain reaction. Donaldson began his work more than a year before the first Hanford reactor started, so reactor coolant was not available. Instead he used equipment that in today's high-tech world would seem ridiculous. He scrounged an X-ray machine designed for hospital use and, in a meticulously planned program, began delivering measured amounts of X-ray to salmon eggs, fingerlings, and spawning adults.

About the time Donaldson was searching for the old X-ray machine in Seattle, the Army was also seeking information on the impact of the pollutants released from Hanford's tall smokestacks. To study wind patterns, workers at Hanford burned oil at the processing plant construction site to generate smoke and traced it for miles across the desert. They even built temporary stacks to release sulfur-dioxide gas to try to trace air currents. That was not successful; the gas was hard to trace and threatened to asphyxiate workers.

By January 1944, Lt. Col. Matthias was asking Phil E. Church about wind dispersion of gasses. Church, among other things, taught meteorology to classes of young Navy sailors and marines at the University of Washington. (I was a sailor in one of his classes.)

He was at Hanford the next month urging construction of a 350-foot meteorological tower to study wind patterns that would control the dispersal of the contaminants. Illustrating how little was still known about the separation process, Matthias noted in a February 21,

1944, diary entry that Church "did not know and apparently no one else knows what opportunities there will be to control the discharge from the stacks" at the separation plants. If it were possible to hold the discharges and wait for favorable winds, Matthias could see the need for precise studies. But if the discharges were not controllable, what was the point of spending money on a tower?

As it turned out, plutonium separation was done batch by batch and it was possible to control discharges, which was done several times. Church got the 350-foot tower.

He was most worried about winter weather at Hanford when temperature inversions would hold cold air and contaminants close to the ground. Summer breezes and better circulation would carry emissions off site. In those days, the primary concern was exposure to Hanford workers. Concern for people off site, the so-called down-winders, came many years later.

Church and Donaldson probably knew each other on the university campus. With both pledged to secrecy, however, it's doubtful either knew what the other was doing for the atomic-bomb project. Church may have had an idea of how his work fit in. He visited Hanford several times and may have known the gasses to be dispersed were radioactively contaminated. Donaldson, confined to his campus laboratory and the hospital X-ray machine, wasn't briefed on the project until the spring of 1945, when testing fish in tanks of actual coolant began at Hanford.

The decision to pass river water through the reactors just once and then return it to the river was unprecedented. The first reactor in Chicago was so small it did not require cooling. A pilot reactor being built in Tennessee, a little bigger, would be air cooled. But with the big reactors planned for Hanford, getting rid of the heat was crucial. Most of the energy released in the fission of uranium is in the form of heat, enough to destroy a big reactor if not dissipated.

Engineers with DuPont favored helium gas as coolant. One of the Met Lab scientists proposed a liquid metal, bismuth. Eugene Wigner, also at the Met Lab, was arguing for plain old water.

All had problems. Bismuth and helium would be hard to obtain quickly in the needed quantities. Use of high-pressure helium would require developing compressors and building a vacuum-tight structure.

Water would absorb neutrons, perhaps enough to prevent a chain reaction. You'll remember k, the multiplication factor of neutrons produced in the fission of a uranium atom. To sustain a chain reaction, k must be more than 1. In the world's first chain reaction in Chicago only a few weeks earlier, k had been barely above 1. DuPont worried that water inside the reactor would steal enough neutrons to kill the reaction.

Wigner pointed out that the quality of both graphite and uranium had improved markedly since Enrico Fermi and his crew had painstakingly put together that first reactor. Wigner staked his argument—and his reputation—on the hope that those improvements would boost k to the point where the capture of neutrons by water would not be a serious problem. Wigner was ready with a design for a water-cooled reactor. It called for drilling tubes through a huge graphite block, lining the tubes with aluminum and filling the tubes with uranium fuel canned in aluminum. Cooling water would be pumped through the gap between the cans and the lining of the tubes.

A month after Brig. Gen. Groves had approved the Hanford site, reactor design was still delayed waiting for a decision on cooling. Groves was pushing impatiently for an end to what he considered scientific dithering.

The decision finally fell to Crawford Greenewalt, 41, the chemical engineer who had managed DuPont's nylon program in the 1930s. As DuPont's technical director for the Hanford project, he was in the often uncomfortable spot of keeping peace among unhappy Met Lab scientists, DuPont engineers, and the Army.

Greenewalt was worried that water might leak through the cans and corrode the uranium or might flash to steam in a plugged tube, causing explosions. But he worried more about the problems with helium, so finally, in late February 1943, he decided on water cooling—a curiously old-fashioned method in this first-of-a-kind device.

Water cools a lot of machines in everyday life, such as automobile engines where water heated by the engine cools as it passes through the radiator and then returns to cool the engine again. Greenewalt's decision, approved by the Army, was to run the cooling water through the reactor just once, retain it for a few hours in an open-air basin, and then return it to the river. The "cooling" stay in the basin, initially about six hours, would allow shorter-lived fission products to decay, lessening total radioactivity to about 1/20th of what it had been. But there would still be activity in the water and it would still be much warmer than river water when it was released from pipelines in the deepest part of the river.

Gen. Groves had grown up in Seattle and was aware of the near-sacred status of salmon. Soon after he had selected the Hanford site, Groves talked with the Army officer who had been in charge of building fish ladders at Bonneville Dam in the 1930s. The officer, apparently remembering the ferocity of aroused salmon fishermen, told Groves: "Whatever you may accomplish, you will incur the everlasting enmity of the entire Northwest if you harm a single scale on a single salmon." The warning, Groves wrote, "made a lasting impression on me."

The Army probably was genuinely concerned about salmon, but the overriding concern was to keep the reactors from overheating. The term "meltdown" was not yet in common use but that is what could have happened to a Hanford reactor if cooling had somehow failed. The reactor could not have exploded like a bomb, but runaway heat could melt the uranium fuel and steam explosions could breach the building, blowing dangerously radioactive debris across the countryside. Unlike modern power reactors, Hanford's wartime reactors did not have containment shells to prevent release of radioactive debris in case of accident.

DuPont's engineers were understandably super-cautious. They designed three cooling systems, the primary system and two backups; one of the backup systems was used at least once. The cooling systems turned out to be among the biggest expenses of Hanford construction.

The primary system was pumps driven by electric motors, making Hanford the biggest consumer of electricity flowing from Grand Coulee and Bonneville Dams. The system drew water from the river and pumped it to holding tanks, then through thousands of pipes and valves and finally through the tubes in the reactor core.

If the electrical supply should fail, the first backup relied on steam power to generate electricity to run the pumps. That entailed maintaining steam pressure in boilers heated by coal fires when the reactors were operating. And it kept Matthias searching for coal, also needed to heat temporary living quarters for construction workers at Hanford. In a November 17, 1943, diary entry while B Reactor was still in early stages of construction, Matthias estimated the project would need 500,000 tons of coal over the next 20 months. (That mention of 20 months, probably just an estimate for planning purposes, seems eerily predictive. Twenty months from late 1943 would take it to August 1945, the month atomic bombs fell on Japan and the war ended.) On February 23, 1944, he noted, "Still looking for sources of coal nearby." He personally checked coal mines in Washington state but decided none of the deposits could produce as much as Hanford needed. Coal eventually arrived by rail from out of state.

The second cooling backup method, called the Last Ditch Cooling System by the engineers, consisted of elevated storage tanks (the water towers you see in old photographs of the wartime reactors). The idea was that if all else failed, gravity would send water through the reactor as the tanks drained. Pipelines connected the tanks, spaced six miles apart, to each other and to each reactor so that all the tanks could be used for one stricken reactor if necessary.

As far as I know, the Last Ditch Cooling System was never needed, but the coal-fired steam-driven generators were used at least once. That story involves one of the stranger weapons of the war in the Pacific—the fire balloons released in Japan to drift to America.

The Japanese Army began releasing the balloons in November 1944 from the east coast of Honshu Island. The balloons, made of tough, impermeable paper, were hydrogen filled and 30 feet in diameter. The Japanese were among the first to recognize the high-altitude river of air that flows eastward across the Pacific (now called the jet stream). When the balloons began arriving along the West Coast, Americans unaware of the jet stream assumed they must have been launched by submarines offshore. Of about 9,000 fire balloons launched, 300 were found in North America, one as far east as the outskirts of Detroit.

A control system fired a charge of gunpowder to drop a bomb after three days, the Japanese estimate for the cross-Pacific trip. Some were incendiary, some high explosive.

On March 10, 1945, one of the balloons hit a power line about 35 miles south of the reactors, briefly interrupting power to the cooling pumps and shutting down a reactor. Steam-generated power automatically restarted the pumps almost immediately to cool the reactor, still dangerously hot.

Years later, Matthias recalled that the power interruption, less than a second, "was enough to shut down the one reactor we had operating that day. The [backup] we put in took over. We were delighted. We'd never tested it before. I used to say we were shut down by direct enemy action."

The balloons did take a tragic toll a couple of months later. On May 5, 1945, one of the last fire bombs launched by Japan killed a woman and five children during a church outing near Klamath Falls, Oregon. They were the only known casualties of this strange weapon.

While the radioactive materials in the cooling water being returned to the Columbia River were not visible, the complicated job of extracting plutonium from irradiated uranium slugs produced highly visible gasses pouring from 200-foot-high stacks. It blew with the wind or on cold days settled to the ground.

Leona Marshall Libby described how "great plumes of brown fumes blossomed above the concrete canyons," the strange-looking buildings where plutonium was extracted chemically from the dangerous, highly radioactive mix of uranium and fission products. The first "concrete canyon" was the T Plant, 875 feet long, about 90 feet wide, and about 100 feet from top to bottom, although about 20 feet was below ground level. Construction workers who had no idea what this odd-shaped building would be used for nicknamed it the "Queen Mary" for the British ocean liner that, by 1944, had been converted to a troop ship.

T Plant resembled a long, narrow canyon with a roof. It was windowless and contained a series of cells, mostly below ground level, separated by thick concrete walls. Operators in the gallery above the cells used remotely controlled tools to perform the tedious step-by-step chemical extraction of plutonium developed by Glenn Seaborg's group in 1943—a stupendous billion-times scale-up from laboratory procedures in test tubes. Operators pumped the mix from cell to cell, the plutonium concentration increasing with each step.

Workers who kidded about the Queen Mary would have been incredulous if they had known that each ton of irradiated uranium

T Plant, where plutonium was separated from uranium. Workers, who had no idea what they were building, nicknamed it the Queen Mary.
Department of Energy.

that went in one end of the Queen Mary contained only about eight ounces of plutonium—the objective of the whole Hanford project. Seaborg wrote later that for a while at least "tons and tons of material were shipped in to Hanford but nothing ever seemed to come out."

The fact that everything worked in the Queen Mary should have been viewed as a near miracle of engineering. The chemical process of coaxing bits of plutonium from tons of irradiated fuel slugs had been gleaned from experiments using less than a milligram (0.00003 ounce) of plutonium back in the Met Lab. Yet it did work. However, because of strict secrecy, hardly anyone knew about it until the bomb ended the war. In the frightening new atomic age the "miracle" remained largely unknown, except to those who had worked on it.

Tons of irradiated uranium from B Reactor arrived at T Plant by rail, a 10-mile trip. Operators using remotely controlled tools grappled the slugs from the heavy transport tanks into the first cell where the aluminum cans encasing the uranium slugs were dissolved. Then nitric acid dissolved the uranium itself, changing the metallic slugs into a slurry and releasing radioactive fission products that until now had been locked in the uranium. This material, some worrisome, some not, went out the stacks as the brown fumes.

The most abundant of the worrisome fission products was iodine-131, a radioactive form of the iodine needed and concentrated by thyroid glands in humans and animals. Unfortunately, the thyroid can't tell the difference between iodine and its radioactive cousin. Exposure to I-131 may increase the danger of thyroid disease, including thyroid cancer.

Medical personnel at Hanford were aware of the problem. Soon after T Plant started up, they asked Army guards to occasionally shoot and bring in coyotes. Sure enough, I-131 concentrations were increasing in coyote thyroids. The iodine-131 was settling on the foliage of sagebrush, which was eaten by rabbits, and the coyotes ate the rabbits.

Iodine-131 was soon recognized as the most critical airborne contaminant released at Hanford. It could enter the bloodstream of either humans or animals by inhalation or ingestion of contaminated food.

The biggest worry was that I-131 could enter the human food chain in milk if cows grazed on contaminated pasture. Children younger than 10 at the time of exposure are considered the most vulnerable.

Secrecy of the project and concern about alarming the public led to some unusual—and secret—methods. At one point, Hanford volunteers used jeeps to chase cows in farm lands downwind from the project, trying unsuccessfully to lasso them. When the exhausted cows finally stopped running, the "cowboys" would hold a radiation monitor against the thyroid in the animal's neck. Even this primitive test showed I-131 concentrations. In a more methodical approach, DuPont technicians began installing monitors throughout the Hanford project and in the surrounding towns and farms. Measurements showed detectable levels of I-131 soon after plutonium separation began.

The best way to reduce I-131 in the emissions was to increase the cooling time for the uranium slugs after they were removed from the reactor and before they went to the T Plant. The longer the slugs cooled, the greater the drop in radioactivity due to decay of shorter-lived fission products, including I-131. The extended cooling time, however, conflicted with the relentless pressure for production speed.

By the summer of 1945, three reactors—B, D, and F—and two Queen Marys—T and B Plants—were operating. The Queen Marys could process the uranium slugs faster than the reactors could produce them, so plutonium separation sometimes had to stop, adding to the pressure to shorten cooling times. The first batches of uranium slugs cooled for about 30 days. Under pressure, the time appears sometimes to have been as short as 15 days. (With less pressure after the war ended, cooling time was as long as 90 days.)

The cooling took advantage of the half-life of radioactive materials. Each fission product has a distinct half-life; Hanford's fuel slugs had materials with half-lives ranging from seconds to many years. Iodine-131's half-life is about eight days. In 15 days, about two half-lives, its radioactivity will decrease to about one-fourth of the original amount. Aging for a little over a month, about four half-lives for I-131, reduced its radioactivity to about one-sixteenth

Hanford, 1945. B Reactor is the blocky building between the elevated water tanks. The long building was for handling and treating cooling water. The Columbia River is in the background.
Department of Energy.

of the original. But that one-sixteenth would still go out the stack when the uranium dissolved.

At least twice during the summer of 1945—once when plutonium was needed for a test explosion in New Mexico and again for the Nagasaki bomb—cooling time was reduced to shorter times than DuPont thought advisable.

On several occasions, dissolving a batch of slugs was postponed for several hours after warnings from meteorologists of unfavorable weather conditions. During warm weather, processing shifted to night when wind conditions were better. Still, these precautions were aimed at protecting the workers, getting the releases off site, and relying on dilution by wind.

The biggest and worst release at Hanford was the highly radioactive liquid waste that was pumped to underground steel tanks near the Queen Marys. Processing each ton of uranium slugs produced 10,000

gallons of liquid waste containing fission products and chemicals used to dissolve the aluminum cans and slugs, as well as the dissolved uranium and aluminum.

In wartime, stainless steel was almost impossible to obtain in the quantities needed for the tanks, so they were built quickly with a single shell of carbon steel. Miles from the river and atop a plateau with 200 feet of almost dry soil beneath them, the tanks were considered safe, temporary storage. Depending on how you define temporary, the tanks served that purpose well. They were out of sight and isolated from living things for years. But military demands for plutonium during the Cold War of the 1950s and 1960s took precedence over finding a permanent solution. Hanford ended up with a much greater volume of waste than anyone anticipated in 1945 and temporary storage turned into semi-permanent. Twenty or so years after the end of the war, tank waste was leaking into Hanford's dry soil and drifting toward the river, causing problems we still face today.

The amount of radioactivity released to the river, to the atmosphere, and stored in the tanks is stunning by today's standards. Perhaps the most understandable unit of measurement is the curie, which describes the rate at which a radioactive material releases particles and loses energy as it decays—the intensity or strength of radioactivity in a material. The curie is not a direct measure of hazard from radiation. Hazard depends on such things as the type of radiation, how much is received by body tissues, and the age of the recipient.

When T Plant dissolved its first set of uranium slugs in December 1944, fumes carried 1,700 curies out the stacks. The first two years of operation released 420,000 curies of iodine-131 to the atmosphere. For comparison, only 15 curies of iodine-131 escaped during America's most serious commercial nuclear accident at the Three Mile Island power plant in Pennsylvania in 1979 when the supply of cooling water failed and half of the reactor core actually melted. Although no deaths or injuries were attributed to Three Mile Island, there were casualties in the devastating Chernobyl accident in what was then the Soviet Republic of Ukraine in 1986, history's worst nuclear accident. An estimated 100 million curies, including a wide variety of radioactive materials, were released.

I worked with Lauren Donaldson in the 1960s, more than 20 years after he began radiation studies on salmon. He told me that when the Army was pushing for increased production at Hanford, coolant from the three wartime reactors carried 900 to 1,000 curies a day into the Columbia River. This was confirmed in the 1980s when the Department of Energy released thousands of documents detailing operations at Hanford. An estimated 40,000 curies went into the river in Hanford's first two years of operation, a time when no one had a very good idea about safe limits of these discharges. The whole project was still secret, so those downstream who swam or fished or drank the water had no inkling of what was in the river. By late 1946, with wartime urgency gone, releases had diminished to about 50 curies a day. But the discharges to the river in Hanford's first few years of operation were dwarfed during the Cold War. During 1956-1965 with as many as eight reactors operating at Hanford, an average of 10,000 to 12,000 curies a day were released into the river.

There was a wide variety of radioactive material in the coolant. Minerals that occur naturally in river water may capture a neutron while passing through the reactor, forming unstable, radioactive forms. Neutrons also could activate chemicals used to treat the water before it went through the reactor. And uranium slugs in the reactor occasionally ruptured and released hazardous fission products into the cooling water and the river.

Months after Hanford's reactors began discharging coolant into the river, Donaldson was still radiating fish with the antiquated X-ray machine in his UW lab. In May 1945, Matthias showed up to discuss moving the research to Hanford, to study fish swimming in tanks of actual reactor coolant. On that visit, Matthias told Donaldson why the fish studies were needed, apparently the first that Donaldson knew about the atom-bomb program or that the Army was involved. (His contract was with the Office of Scientific Research and Development.)

They agreed Donaldson would continue to direct the project and Richard F. Foster, a member of Donaldson's team at UW, would join DuPont to run the studies at Hanford.

There was unhappiness at the university about Donaldson's mysterious project. Matthias had received an irate call from UW's director of fisheries who had just found out about the project. Matthias's diary noted that Donaldson asked for a letter to the university because "the president of the university and other people concerned have no idea" what he was doing or why.

A month or so after the war ended, Matthias visited the university again to explain the work more fully to Lee Paul Sieg, university president. Matthias's diary noted that Sieg seemed appreciative "as they have felt for a long time that the work was being done with little regard for administrative" needs. Sieg and William F. Thompson, director of the school of fisheries, "asked that we permit Donaldson to devote at least half his time to teaching. We agreed," Matthias noted.

As Foster set up his work at Hanford, he began following the health of fish in tanks containing various concentrations of reactor coolant. Almost all the fish in warm, undiluted coolant from reactors died. But almost all survived in water diluted to what was believed to be the average concentration and temperature in the river downstream from the reactor's outlets. There were also problems with parasites and disease, probably caused by elevated temperatures of the coolant.

Foster issued almost daily bulletins for workers at Hanford. Leona Marshall Libby, working at B Reactor and apparently amused by the reports, wrote that the bulletins might read, "The fish spent a good night and appear to be feeling well." Or "The fish are doing somewhat poorly today." Or "The fish are much better and are even jumping out of the water."

As a reporter for the *Tri-City Herald* in 1951, I visited Foster's testing station at Hanford. He told me his group had not been able to detect any harmful effects on the river itself, although fish near the reactors had picked up radioactive traces—but were still safe to eat. He said most of the radioactivity was in the fish kidneys and livers, parts not usually consumed.

Foster told me that harmful effects did not appear in salmon fingerlings until the concentration in the tanks increased to one part coolant to 20 parts river water—a five times greater concentration than found in the river.

The story I wrote seems a bit innocent today. It was picked up by the Associated Press and published by several papers in the region, an indication of strong interest in Hanford's effect on the river.

Foster was limited in what he could tell me because of the strict secrecy the Atomic Energy Commission (AEC) still clamped on almost everything about the Hanford project—six years after the end of the war and two years after the Soviets had exploded their own atomic bomb. As was customary in those years, I was escorted on the Hanford reservation by an AEC representative.

A scientific paper by another biologist at Hanford about that time reported that concentrations of radioactivity in fish in the river were many times greater than that in the water itself. This was due to the traces of radioactivity in algae eaten by the fish, which then became concentrated in fish tissue. The principle is well known today but was a surprise at the time, indicating the early stage of knowledge of radiation effects on aquatic animals. That report, like others, remained secret for many years.

The Cold War's increased demand for weapons plutonium added greatly to Hanford's total radioactive releases to both the river and the atmosphere. An estimated 32 million curies went out the stacks of the plutonium-separation plants from 1944 to 1971, despite improvements that reduced releases. Most of the airborne releases were not particularly hazardous to living things. Iodine-131, representing only about 2 percent of total airborne releases, accounted for almost all of the radiation dose potentially received by downwinders. Today, after more than 1,000 half-lives, the I-131 is essentially gone.

As many as eight reactors with single-pass cooling were operating simultaneously at Hanford during much of the Cold War. An estimated 113 million curies of ionizing radiation went into the river from 1944 through 1971, when the old reactors were shut down. There were even traces of radioactivity in shellfish harvested along the coast near the mouth of the Columbia River.

Thankfully, the days of near feverish production at Hanford are long gone and the river has largely recovered. The Washington State Health Department says radioactivity in the river today is predominantly from natural sources, although sediment along the shoreline near Hanford still contains detectable levels of several radioactive materials. The water downstream is safe for drinking, swimming, and fishing.

Interestingly, the river preserves a record of Hanford's Cold War contamination buried in the sediment behind McNary Dam, about 65 miles downstream from the reactors. The dam was completed in 1954 while all eight reactors were still operating at Hanford. Sediment washing into the Columbia from the Yakima, Snake, and Walla Walla Rivers accumulates about a foot a year behind the dam. Geologists from the University of Washington in the 1970s analyzed cores retrieved from that sediment. Short-lived radiation was gone but several radionuclides with half-lives of 30 or more years provide a record of Hanford's Cold War activity.

Franklin T. Matthias
Department of Energy.

Chapter 10

The Bomb

I t was a plain wooden box, 14 inches square and a little taller, with a handle fastened to the top. But the contents, enclosed in a stainless-steel flask, wrapped in leak-proof material and suspended with shock absorbers—perhaps strips cut from an old rubber inner tube—were precious: the first Hanford-produced plutonium.

The box wouldn't have been very heavy. There were only 100 grams (about 3½ ounces) of plutonium in the flask. It was the first tiny product of the Hanford project that in more than two years had taken hundreds of thousands of acres of land, consumed hundreds of millions of dollars in materials and equipment, and required the labor of tens of thousands of workers.

The DuPont Company had transferred the plutonium to the Army at Hanford the day before, and this day, February 3, 1945, it began its trip to a secret laboratory in New Mexico where scientists desperately needed to study the characteristics of this strange new metal.

Lt. Col. Matthias and a security guard drove the plutonium along the Columbia River to Portland, apparently in the front seat between them. In Portland Matthias carried the box aboard the train for the overnight trip to Los Angeles. He remembered in later years that the box looked like something any traveler might be carrying, nothing to attract attention.

Despite its scary reputation, the plutonium was not particularly dangerous to transport that way, unless, of course, a traffic or railroad accident had ruptured the container. Plutonium's radioactive emissions are easily shielded, but the emissions would have been warming the box's interior.

In Los Angeles, Matthias handed the box to a young Army officer who would take it—still by railroad—to the Los Alamos laboratory where scientists were working on designs for atomic bombs. Space on passenger trains was tight during wartime and the officer had only managed to get an upper berth for the trip. Matthias remembered telling the officer that the material in the box was very important and had cost hundreds of millions of dollars. Surprised and impressed, the officer harangued a ticket agent until he got a locked compartment for the overnight trip.

Strange as it may seem now, the whole plutonium project had come close to being shut down—including serious consideration of stopping construction at Hanford—almost a year before Matthias carried that first bit of plutonium in the wooden box.

The problem was an impurity in reactor-produced plutonium. The impurity had been predicted in theory but amounts of plutonium produced in laboratories had been so small that determining its extent was difficult. When the first grams of plutonium from the pilot plant in Tennessee arrived at Los Alamos, however, test results were disconcerting. Plutonium produced in Hanford's reactors would contain the same impurity, causing serious doubt that a plutonium bomb would be possible.

Design of the bomb itself, known as the gun assembly, was well along by this time. The basic idea was simple. Portions of fissile material, neither enough to form a critical mass, would be placed in each

The initial Hanford shipment was plutonium nitrate, a syrupy semi-liquid that looked a little like brown molasses. It was converted to solid metal at Los Alamos. Subsequent wartime shipments of plutonium nitrate from Hanford to Los Alamos were partly dried, sealed in special cans, and rode in Army ambulances in armed convoys. The route went through Boise to Salt Lake City, where the precious material was transferred at Fort Douglas to another convoy to complete the trip. A plutonium-finishing plant began operating at Hanford in 1949 and produced plutonium metal during the Cold War.

end of a gun barrel. (Designers began working with an anti-aircraft gun barrel acquired from the Navy.) Using conventional explosives, one portion, the "bullet," would be fired down the barrel into the other, the "target." As the two slammed together, they would form a critical mass, triggering an uncontrolled chain reaction—an atomic explosion. Designers had assumed the gun assembly would work for both plutonium and highly enriched uranium, which was being manufactured at Oak Ridge, Tennessee.

The impurity, plutonium-240, was an isotope of the desired bomb material, plutonium-239, and an inevitable byproduct of producing plutonium in a reactor. The problem was that plutonium-240 fissions spontaneously, posing the danger of starting a chain reaction prematurely—a fizzle. Admittedly, a fizzle would still be a nasty explosion, but nowhere near the power of an atomic bomb.

By the summer of 1944, scientists at Los Alamos had decided the gun design could not slam portions of plutonium together fast enough—even at 3,000 feet per second—to prevent a fizzle. The two versions of plutonium were such close cousins there was no feasible way to separate them.

Brig. Gen. Groves called an emergency meeting in Chicago on July 17. Both military and scientific brass were present to discuss the quandary: Should they continue construction at Hanford, taking the chance that a plutonium bomb was not possible? Or should Hanford be shut down, running the risk of not having plutonium if, seemingly against the odds, a new design for a plutonium bomb could be ready in time for use in the war?

Groves knew of preliminary work at Los Alamos on a different design for a plutonium bomb. Instead of slamming two chunks of fissionable material together, the idea was to use conventional explosives to suddenly compress a sphere of plutonium into a critical mass. Work on the approach—implosion—had been low priority and to that point not particularly successful.

Col. Kenneth D. Nichols was at the meeting in Chicago and wrote that "the summer and fall of 1944 marked the low point of our expectations." In fact, he said if the project had not been protected by super secrecy, it could have been killed by Congress. Charges that a plutonium bomb was impossible would have been "hard to disprove as our troubles continued during the third quarter of 1944."

The decision fell to Groves. He decided that construction would continue at Hanford at the same urgent pace. He ordered more men and resources poured into the project at Los Alamos to design an implosion bomb, an idea with almost no engineering experience behind it. If he worried about the possible waste of millions of dollars at Hanford—and of a postwar scandal—he didn't show it or admit it in later years.

Instead of joining two subcritical masses as in the gun design, the implosion idea was to crush a subcritical mass of plutonium metal so quickly and violently that its density doubled almost instantly. The mass would still contain the same number of atoms, but crowded in half the volume, making it supercritical.

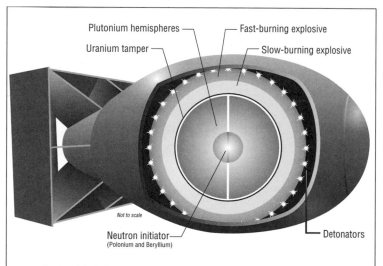

Plutonium hemispheres — Fast-burning explosive
Uranium tamper — Slow-burning explosive

Not to scale

Neutron initiator — Detonators
(Polonium and Beryllium)

A greatly simplified sketch shows the key parts of an implosion bomb. Detonators trigger a shaped explosion that almost instantaneously crushes the plutonium, the initiator releases a flood of neutrons to jump-start the reaction, and the uranium tamper reflects neutrons back into the plutonium.

WSU Press.

The idea was sound in theory, but actually building an implosion bomb was an engineering nightmare. The core of plutonium would be spherical because a sphere, presenting the least surface for a given volume, would best minimize the escape of neutrons as the core imploded. The crushing force exerted on the sphere had to be almost perfectly uniform—exerted simultaneously over the entire exterior surface of the sphere. And it had to be a powerful, almost instantaneous jolt.

Experiments detonating conventional explosives wrapped around spheres—common metals were substituted for plutonium—disturbed the quiet in an isolated canyon at Los Alamos early in 1945 as scientists studied implosion. For a while the experiments were consuming up to a ton a day of high-performance explosives.

The problem was that a typical TNT explosion creates a convex pressure wave. When the wave impinges a sphere, its leading edge strikes part of the sphere's surface before the rest of the surface is affected, spoiling a uniform compression. Somehow they needed to apply uniform pressure to the entire sphere's surface at precisely the same time.

The answer was "shaped" explosives developed earlier in the war to penetrate armor on tanks. Instead of focusing pressure waves to penetrate armor, the aim here was to shape them to exert pressure on the entire surface of the plutonium sphere simultaneously. By combining fast-burning high explosives with slower burning explosives, the pressure wave could be manipulated, somewhat similar to the way a lens bends light waves. Detonators would trigger fast-burning outer blocks of explosive. As the convex pressure wave moved toward the core, embedded blocks of slow-burning explosive would slow the wave's leading edge, bending it into a concave shape that would impact a sphere's surface uniformly. To reduce loss of neutrons as the plutonium core imploded, it was wrapped in a layer of natural uranium to act as a neutron reflector. Additionally, rather than depend on stray neutrons to begin a chain reaction when the sphere imploded, the design included an initiator to provide a sudden flood of neutrons to jump start the reaction.

Ideas for the initiator reached back a few years. In 1932, when James Chadwick was trying to identify the "mystery radiation" produced by a mixture of polonium and beryllium, he identified the radiation as neutrons. Chadwick was at Los Alamos in 1944 and 1945 and helped design an initiator that would provide a burst of neutrons from a mixture of polonium and beryllium.

The initiator was embedded in a hollowed-out section of the plutonium sphere (which was actually two hemispheres fitted together) with the polonium and beryllium separated. At the point of maximum squeeze, the two would mix to release the flood of neutrons, providing the jump start.

In theory, the complicated device should work. But it included so many innovations and inventions that Groves ordered a full-scale test—an atomic explosion. It was a tough decision because Hanford was only beginning to produce plutonium and a test would require a bomb-size quantity of the precious material.

In the meantime, Groves decided there was no need to test the gun design for the uranium-235 bomb. His confidence was based on the military's long experience with artillery and gun barrels—and on a hair-raising experiment at Los Alamos by Otto Frisch. (Frisch and his aunt, Lise Meitner, were the first to realize in 1939 that German physicists had unwittingly split the uranium atom.)

Otto Frisch's wartime identification badge photo. *Los Alamos National Laboratory.*

Frisch's experiment was aimed at learning how much uranium-235 would be necessary for a bomb. Up to that point, the quantity was known only in theory. Using uranium-235 delivered from the Tennessee plants by late 1944, Frisch arranged the uranium so that the central portion was missing, leaving a hole in the middle. The missing material kept the uranium sub-critical.

Then, in a structure 10 feet high that looked a little like a guillotine, the uranium from the "hole" was suspended above the rest of the uranium. Utilizing gravity, he dropped the uranium through the hole. In the split second that it passed through the hole, instruments detected a flood of neutrons and a burst of heat in what Frisch described as "a sort of stifled explosion." The experiment, nicknamed "Tickling the Dragon's Tail" by Frisch's fellow scientists, not only provided valuable information on the necessary quantity for a uranium bomb, but boosted confidence in the gun design.

Groves's decision against a test of the gun design, meaning the first uranium bomb would be used in war, probably was influenced by the fact that a test would have used up the uranium-235 on hand. It would have taken at least a couple of months to make enough for another bomb.

With Groves's ultra-strict compartmentalization of information, Matthias had no official word about the upcoming test of the plutonium bomb. But in the summer of 1945 he had plenty of hints it was imminent. Col. John Lansdale, chief of security for the Manhattan Project, had asked Matthias to help write a cover story about "an explosion" in the New Mexico desert. The proposed news release reported the explosion of an ammunition dump noting that there were no injuries or damage outside the dump. The "phony story," as Matthias called it, was actually released after the test.

On July 12, Groves and two top civilian officials of the Manhattan Project, Vannevar Bush and James Conant, were at Hanford to tour the facilities before continuing to Los Alamos. Matthias had little doubt they were on their way to a test. "I said to Groves, 'Hey, I'd like to go down with you to see the test.' And he said 'What test? How are you supposed to know?'"

Groves turned him down, adding that Col. Nichols would not be permitted to witness the test either. He told Matthias: "I'm not going to let you or Nichols go because you are running production. If we lost you it would be a lot worse for the program than if I got killed."

At the Los Alamos lab, after months of near-frantic work, worries, failed trials, and dead ends, even doubts whether the implosion design would work, a core of Hanford-made plutonium was ready

> Matthias arranged a lunch at the Pasco Naval Air Station while Groves, Conant (president of Harvard University), and Bush were at Hanford. They were introduced by the code names they used for the atomic-bomb project.
>
> Matthias remembered: "I was sitting next to a young Air Corps officer who kept looking at Conant and finally said to me, 'You know, I swear to God that guy was my professor at Harvard.' I said 'heck no, of course not.' He was convinced [he recognized Conant], but we never told him."

for the test. On July 12, the day Groves was visiting Hanford, Philip Morrison, 29, helped insert two hemispheres of plutonium into separate carrying cases. He and Paul C. Aebersold, 35, loaded the cases into the back seat of an Army sedan.

Then, with Morrison and Aebersold seated on each side of the historic cargo, with a driver and guard in the front seat and escorted by armed soldiers, they began the 210-mile trip from Los Alamos to the test site, a corner of the Army's Alamogordo bombing range.

Morrison was a physics instructor recruited to the atomic-bomb project from the University of Illinois. In later years he was a prominent critic of the Cold War nuclear arms race and worked to control and eliminate nuclear weapons. Aebersold, responsible at Los Alamos for radiation safety, became an authority on peaceful uses of nuclear energy. During that trip, however, they were

Philip Morrison helped transport plutonium for the nuclear test in New Mexico in 1945.
Massachusetts Institute of Technology.

If you hold a lump of metallic plutonium in your hand, it's not only surprisingly heavy but feels warm. As plutonium slowly decays, its atoms emit alpha particles that lose energy rapidly as they collide with other particles. The lost energy is converted to heat. Alpha particles, consisting of two protons and two neutrons bound together, are energetic but have little penetrating power and are stopped by healthy skin or even a sheet of paper.

most likely concerned with the steps of putting the device together—joining the core with high explosives, detonators, the initiator, and the shell to enclose it, all of which were arriving separately at the test site.

Years of hard work, inventions, hopes, and doubts all came together with a successful test at 5:30 a.m. on July 16, 1945. In fact, the explosive yield from 13 pounds of plutonium was the equivalent of about 20,000 tons of TNT, more powerful than expected. The flash at dawn was seen for 150 miles, the sound heard for 200 miles, and the shock wave rattled windows 100 miles away. The Alamogordo Air Base, answering inquiries, issued the "news" release Matthias had helped write. The story was used widely in the Southwest but largely ignored in the rest of the country. Matthias's personal diary on that day did not mention the test.

Almost seven years later, as a young reporter for the *Tri-City Herald*, I witnessed a nuclear explosion at the Nevada Test Site. Unlike that first trial, full of uncertainty whether the bomb would work and what unexpected damage it might cause, atomic testing had become as routine as possible for a device that had destroyed two Japanese cities.

This one, on April 22, 1952, was a full-scale media event. The Atomic Energy Commission, which had assumed responsibility for nuclear weapons from the Army, invited more than 200 newspaper, radio, newsreel, and television reporters.

The following is an excerpt from the story I wrote that day:

The author writing his report of the nuclear test in Nevada in 1952.
Courtesy of the author.

The calm voice coming over the loudspeaker said: 'Minus one minute. Put on goggles or face away from the target area.' Sitting about halfway up an outcrop of lava rocks christened News Nob for the test, I squinted up to see the B-50 bomber making its final run and pulled on the dark goggles. It was totally black inside. I tilted back to look directly at the sun and saw only a dull orange blob. The loudspeaker again: 'Remember that the flash of an atomic explosion will cause total and permanent blindness to unprotected eyes.'

The strap on the goggles was too loose so I pushed it against my face. Remembering the warning about blindness, I almost broke my nose snugging up the goggles.

'Thirty seconds. Bombs away.' I noticed with surprise I was breathing faster. I could hear my heart thumping as a deathly quiet settled over News Nob. 'Five seconds.' Cameras started whirring.

As the voice said 'zero' the blackness inside the thick glasses was pierced by a dazzlingly bright glare. I saw a fiery ball which almost instantaneously was flanked by two horizontal sheets of flame. At the same instant a wave of heat struck my face. The heat was frightening; I hadn't expected it. It was as definite as if you opened a hot oven and stuck your face right up to the door.

I counted to three slowly as instructed. But the fiery ball was still so bright even through the goggles that I threw in another count. Then I yanked them off and reached for my camera. The explosion—writhing in silence 3,000 feet above the ground and 10 miles away—was still so bright I had to squint.

As I shot the first pictures, the loudspeaker blared: 'The shock wave will arrive in approximately 30 seconds. Please remain in your places until the shock wave has passed.' But I was so interested shooting pictures that I forgot about the warning and almost had my camera whipped from my hand. The shock had the effect of rocking me backwards.

With the shock came a tremendously loud bang, sounding as though a giant firecracker had gone off six inches from my head in a closed room. The shock wave felt like someone had whacked me hard on the chest with his fist.

The cloud turned pink, then amber with white edges. As it gained altitude, it formed a perfect doughnut shape with the boiling turbulence continuing, with a column of dust and debris pulled up from the ground reaching toward the doughnut. It made a beautiful, if awesome, picture against the dark blue sky. Again, in silence.

I looked around to see how other reporters had taken it. One fellow was trying to change the roll film in his camera. His hands were shaking so he was having a hard time of it. I was just as glad I didn't have to change film. Those who had chosen to look away from the explosion said the flash—for a few seconds fifty times brighter than the sun—threw shadows the wrong way.

That was my first atomic explosion. It wasn't a disappointment. And I pray to God I'll never see one fired to kill.

The bomb dropped that day in Nevada, from 33,000 feet, was pretty much the same design as the test device at Alamogordo and the plutonium bomb dropped on Nagasaki. It weighed about five tons, was five feet in diameter and about 10 feet long. Design improvements in the years since have greatly reduced the size of plutonium warheads.

After the blast, William L. Laurence, the *New York Times* reporter who had been "drafted" by Groves to be historian for the Manhattan Project, estimated the yield at 15,000 to 20,000 tons of TNT. Laurence had witnessed the Nagasaki bombing from a plane accompanying the B-29 that delivered the bomb. His estimate proved accurate; the test that day was about the same size as the Hiroshima and Nagasaki bombs.

William L. Laurence at Nevada test in 1952.
Courtesy of the author.

The test I witnessed was one of eight announced tests that spring, four airdrops and four shot from towers. The United States conducted 928 announced tests in Nevada, most of them underground, from 1951 to 1992.

Lt. Gen. Joseph Swing, then 6th Army commander, had been in a foxhole with troops several miles closer to ground zero than we were. He joined us an hour or so after the blast and cheerfully reported that his only "injury" had been a mouthful of dust when the shock wave hit.

That offhand comment seems almost unbelievable now, as does the fact that we calmly watched the radioactive cloud drift off to the northeast without thinking of the people who lived beneath its path.

Part Four

The Aftermath

The people of Bikini, a coral atoll in the west central Pacific Ocean, may have heard news on the radio of new, terrible bombs that had fallen on Japanese cities. If they did...they couldn't have dreamed how the news would change their world, and very quickly.

February 10, 1946

A mushroom-shaped cloud and water column from the underwater Baker nuclear explosion on July 25, 1946. Photo taken from a tower on Bikini Island, 3.5 miles away. *Department of Energy.*

Marshall Islands

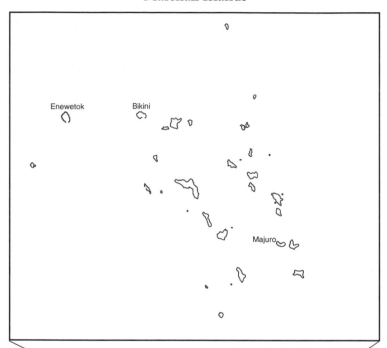

Enewetok

Bikini

Majuro

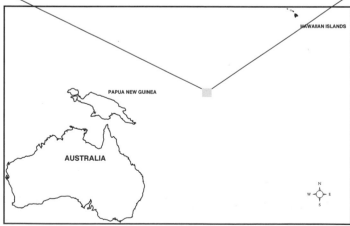

HAWAIIAN ISLANDS

PAPUA NEW GUINEA

AUSTRALIA

N
W E
S

The Marshall Islands, selected by the United States for nuclear testing after the end of World War II.
WSU Press.

Chapter 11

From Japan to Bikini and Enewetak

I t was a hot afternoon and most of the newspaper and radio staff were in shirtsleeves as they scribbled notes or hunched over portable typewriters, firing questions at a young Army officer. Calm and pleasant as usual, Lt. Col. Matthias answered some of the questions; others he smilingly said he was not permitted to answer.

The press conference had been arranged hurriedly after a startling bulletin on the radio at 8:05 a.m. that day, Monday, August 6, 1945: President Truman's announcement that an American plane had dropped a bomb on Hiroshima with "more power than 20,000 tons of TNT...an atomic bomb...a harnessing of the power of the universe." It was a stunning story, finally revealing Hanford's role in a new, terrible weapon.

Reporters from newspapers, wire services, newsreels, and radio networks were crowded in the coffee shop of the Transient Quarters, a hotel-like lodging along the Columbia River in Richland—one of the "hidden" cities being identified publicly for the first time. The room was hazy with tobacco smoke. Off to one side a Teletype printer was clattering. A Women's Army Corps corporal was trying to keep up with three ringing telephones. At one time, there were 15 calls waiting for Lt. Milton R. Cydell, whose job until today had been to suppress news about Hanford. Outside the coffee shop windows lay the Columbia River, powerful, quiet, and still undammed.

The president had identified three sites involved in the Manhattan Project—Hanford, Oak Ridge, and Los Alamos. Henry Stimson, secretary of war, had added that "uranium is the ore essential to the production of the weapon." It was not clear that day that there were two different kinds of bomb, one armed with enriched uranium produced in Tennessee and one with plutonium produced at Hanford—or that the Hiroshima bomb had been armed with uranium.

Matthias told the press conference that the Hanford project's entire contribution to a single bomb would not weigh more than eight or nine pounds. It's interesting to wonder whether Matthias himself knew on that day which bomb had destroyed Hiroshima. He certainly knew that the Tennessee operation had been sending enriched uranium to the bomb designers at the Los Alamos laboratory. But with Gen. Groves's compartmentalization of information there would have been no compelling reason for Matthias to know which bomb had been used first.

Howard Blakeslee, the Associated Press science editor since 1927, came as close to the truth as anyone. He wrote that the Hiroshima bomb was "probably uranium-235."

Matthias had learned of the bombing of Hiroshima just that morning along with the rest of the world, although he had known use of a bomb was imminent. Matthias wouldn't have needed a security reminder but just to be sure, Groves had telephoned him that morning with instructions to make sure reporters and any other visitors remained outside the project fences.

The mood at the press conference was one of relief that the long, bloody war might soon be over, and of awe at the scientific achievement. Reporters at the Richland press conference undoubtedly assumed the first bomb was a Hanford production. (The word "plutonium" had still not reached the public.) Certainly, Hanford workers hearing the news assumed it had been "their" bomb. Matthias's diary entry that day commented that the workers were feeling "great relief... the consciousness that they have contributed to the mechanism that will certainly end the war very soon."

One of those toward the back of the crowded room, listening and scrawling notes with a soft pencil on folded paper, was my father, Hill Williams Sr. It had been two years, five months, and almost two weeks—a time in which the world had changed irretrievably—since Matthias had told him that a huge wartime project would be built nearby and asked that he not write about it.

The next issue of the weekly *Pasco Herald* was several days away so the editor's report was an "extra" headlined with the biggest type he had: IT'S ATOMIC BOMBS! My mother, Ursula Trainor Williams, who had worked at the *Herald* since we children began school, attended the press conference and wrote a color story for that week's paper, headlined:

A Country Editor Goes to a Big Time Press Conference

...having lived for two and a half years practically in the back yard of the famous project, the Country Editor didn't have much to ask. Eyes wandered idly out the window where in the quick closing dusk the river slipped silently by...the river whose power was harnessed to help bring the experiment to successful culmination...rows of telephone booths...a three-network radio hookup...interesting to contemplate [to] what far distant points messages have been transmitted...

Odd to the Country Editor who had known Richland but a few years back...when John Dam's store...Ed Peddicord in the little print shop...the post office...And a fine new high school comprised the town...

The story won a state journalism prize.

News stories reflected continuing secrecy. The next day, the *New York Times* described Hanford's reactors only as "three enormous structures where material is produced," and the separation plants as "huge chemical plants where material is purified." Richland, one of the hitherto secret towns, was described as "on remote banks of the Columbia River in the State of Washington."

Much of the information released the day after the Hiroshima bombing was based on news releases written months before—locked up until now—by William L. Laurence, the *New York Times* writer commandeered as "official reporter" for the Manhattan Project.

As the Richland press conference convened on August 6, Laurence was in a barricaded, air-conditioned building on Tinian Island (where it was already August 7) observing and scribbling notes as the plutonium bomb was assembled. Tinian was the Western Pacific base for B-29 bombers that had been mounting massive raids on Japanese cities for months. Two days later, from a plane accompanying the B-29

The Smyth Report

Less than a week after the Richland press conference, a good deal more information about nuclear bombs became available with publication of the so-called Smyth Report, written by Henry D. Smyth, a physicist at Princeton University. The report, formally known as *Atomic Energy for Military Purposes: A General Account of the Scientific Research and Technical Development That Went into to the Making of Atomic Bombs*, was released August 12, after Hiroshima and Nagasaki were bombed but three days before Japan surrendered.

The Smyth Report used the word "plutonium" to discus Hanford's work. It apparently was the first public use of the word.

About a year earlier Groves had asked Smyth to prepare an account of the science that led to the bombs, intending the report to define what information could be made public without violating national security. The report contained little detail about how the bombs were assembled and detonated. Still, it appalled the British, who thought it revealed too many secrets. Scientists in the Soviet Union, with information from spies in the Manhattan Project, were already developing an atomic weapon. But the Smyth Report, identifying what worked and what didn't work, undoubtedly saved them time.

The Soviets exploded their first atomic bomb—made of plutonium with an implosion design—on August 29, 1949, at the Semipalatinsk Test Site (located in present-day Kazakhstan).

that carried the plutonium bomb, Laurence witnessed the massive explosion over Nagasaki. Japan surrendered August 15.

The unprecedented destruction caused by the bombs dropped on Japan jolted Navy officials, already uncomfortably aware that World War II had seen, for the first time, major warships sunk by aircraft. Hanford was still producing plutonium and both military and congressional leaders wanted to test the new bomb on naval vessels.

In late 1945, just a few months after Japan surrendered, the search began for a test site. It had to be isolated, in an area controlled by the United States, uninhabited or with so few people they could be easily moved out, and with a sheltered anchorage for the target ships.

The people of Bikini, a coral atoll in the west central Pacific Ocean, may have heard on the radio of the new, terrible bombs that had fallen on Japanese cities. If they did, like most of us, they wouldn't

Atoll: A work of millions of years

WSU Press.

From the air an atoll looks like a necklace thrown down carelessly so that even though it may be roughly circular, there are bends and curves as it encloses a lagoon. Dark green islands are bordered on the ocean side by the reef where shallow water is a light, almost fluorescent, green. A white band of surf marks where the reef drops precipitously to the deep blue of the ocean. Beaches glare white on the lagoon side of the islands. The lagoon bottom shelves gradually away from the beaches, changing from a yellowish green to darker green to blue, to depths not more than 200 feet.

A typical atoll began when a volcanic island formed millions of years ago and corals grew a fringing reef. As the volcano died and began to sink beneath the surface, the coral continued to grow, with live corals forming on top of those that died when they sank below the depth where sunlight can penetrate the water.

have grasped the world-changing significance. And they couldn't have dreamed how the news would change their world so quickly.

Bikini Atoll and its people, part of the Marshall Islands captured from the Japanese, had suffered little during World War II. Five Japanese soldiers stationed there as weather observers had committed suicide when American troops landed in 1944. The atoll met the Navy's requirements for tests.

Just six months after the war ended, on February 10, 1946, a Navy officer arrived at Bikini by seaplane to talk with Bikini's leaders. After church services—it was a Sunday—Commander Ben H. Wyatt told them about the bombs that had ended the war.

The meeting would have taken place in an open area in the center of the village with Juda, the elected magistrate, along with ten or so heads of Bikini families seated cross-legged on white coral gravel facing Wyatt, who was standing. Curious women and children would have been watching the unexpected meeting.

Juda, the elected magistrate of the Bikini people.
University of Washington Library Special Collections.

The Navy officer's message was an emotional bombshell. Through an interpreter, Wyatt told the islanders that America needed to test the new bombs further, that the Navy had searched the world and determined that Bikini was the best place for the tests. He asked the Bikini people "for the good of mankind and to end all world wars" to leave their home islands to make way for the tests. He promised the Navy would find them a new home. Wyatt asked that they leave within a week, although the actual move turned out to be several weeks later than that.

You can imagine the shock. Most of the people had lived their entire lives on their atoll. They were skillful sailors and traditionally had visited extended family on other islands. But their village, the land owned by families, and the lagoon that provided fish, were all at Bikini Atoll.

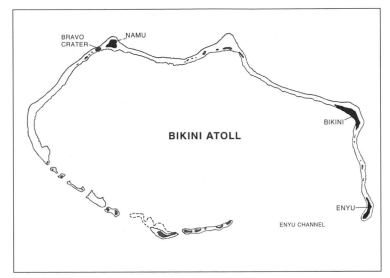

Map of the Bikini Atoll.
WSU Press.

Despite later reports that the Bikinians were happy to cooperate, they probably felt they had little choice. For generations, they had been subject to authoritative colonial governments, first Spain and Germany, and then Japan. Now the conquering Americans were asking them to move. After a discussion among the Bikini men, probably not lasting more than an hour, Juda said they would go.

"Juda was a forceful man; there would have been no great argument" among the Bikinians, Leonard Mason, a University of Hawaii anthropologist, told me in the 1960s.

On March 7, 1946, the 167 Bikini people carried their belongings aboard a Navy landing craft and departed their ancestral home. Some sang songs of farewell, a few wept, but most were silent. The people were taken 125 miles eastward to an uninhabited atoll known as Rongerik where a work party of Navy Seabees and Bikini workers had prepared a new village. Even as the people were preparing to leave Bikini, American ships began arriving with military and scientific personnel to begin test preparations.

Operation Crossroads, a name selected by the Navy, opened on July 1, 1946, with an atomic bomb dropped from a B-29 exploding 520 feet above the target ships in Bikini's lagoon. The second test was detonated 90 feet underwater beneath the target ships on July 25. Both were about the yield of the bombs dropped on Japan. They were the fourth and fifth nuclear explosions in history, after the New Mexico test, Hiroshima, and Nagasaki.

The underwater test was an eye-opener for both scientists and the military. They had assumed tidal flow would clear the lagoon of radioactive contamination fairly quickly. It didn't happen. Instead, plant and animal life in the lagoon took up the radioactive material and retained it. It was a surprising lesson in the early days of the atomic age. And it doomed any hopes of the Bikini people for an early return home.

Mason believed that both the Bikinians and Americans considered the move temporary, "maybe for a year. At that time no one suspected what would happen in the second test."

Jack A. Tobin, an American anthropologist with the government agency set up to administer the Marshall Islands after the war, agreed. "I think it's unlikely they would have left if they knew they could never return," Tobin told me. "I think it was a case of unsophisticated people being asked something they didn't understand."

Support ships moving into the lagoon after the underwater test became contaminated as marine growth attached to the ship's hulls. Levels were worrisome enough that crews were warned not to sleep or work near bulkheads that could be contaminated. Adding to the puzzle, radioactivity in the lagoon rose at night and decreased during the day. It turned out to be caused by vertical movement of contaminated plankton in response to light levels.

A University of Washington group led by Lauren R. Donaldson did much of the research that finally explained what was happening in the lagoon. It had been three years since Donaldson had begun studying radiation effects on Columbia River salmon.

As the Bikini people settled in their new home at Rongerik, ships and men poured into Bikini. Operation Crossroads was not only a

Juda, about 1946.
Courtesy of Jack Niedenthal.

The Navy flew Juda and three other Bikini leaders to Bikini on August 6, a couple of weeks after Operation Crossroads' second test. They were escorted around the atoll for six days.

Juda's oldest son, Rubon, recalled that when his father returned to Rongerik he told his people that Bikini wasn't gone; it was still there. Rubon remembered his father reassuring the family that "The birds and pigs were still alive and running around on the island…the hermit crabs could be seen on the beach. The trees remained intact and continued to blow in the wind. Some of the houses were still standing."

Rubon, relating the story to Jack Niedenthal, an American who has worked with the Bikini people since 1984, added, "And so we stayed hopeful that we would soon return to our islands."

It's understandable that Juda's visit would have been encouraging. The first two shots were near the center of the lagoon, miles from the islands, so there would not yet have been a lot of visible damage. The islands were still there, coconut trees still standing. The lingering radioactivity in the atoll's plant and animal life was not apparent to Juda and only beginning to be understood by the Americans.

The real battering of the Bikini Atoll was still in the future when it was reactivated as a test site for the Bravo hydrogen-bomb blast.

mammoth undertaking—eventually involving 42,000 military and scientific personnel, members of Congress, hundreds of ships and planes, and thousands of experimental animals—but also a media show for 114 newspaper and broadcast representatives from all over the world. There was even a "press headquarters" ship. Seventy damaged or captured warships and small craft were anchored in the target area in the lagoon.

The Bikini people, 125 miles away, heard the blast of the aerial explosion. They knew what it was; some became angry, some wept. It may have been their first realization that they would not be back home quickly.

Both Bikini leaders and Navy officers had doubts about the suitability of Rongerik as a new home. Much smaller than Bikini, its 10 islands comprised less than a third of the dry land on Bikini's 26 islands. The lagoon, important for fishing, was less than a quarter the size of Bikini's. Less than a year after the move, it became obvious why Rongerik had not been inhabited; it simply could not produce enough food for even a small population.

Alarmed Navy officers asked Mason to visit Rongerik. He immediately radioed word of a critical food shortage. The Navy dispatched food supplies as a doctor reported the people were actually nearing starvation.

Navy officials previously had discussed moving the people to another atoll, Ujelang, bigger and uninhabited, and the Bikini leaders, although hesitant about moving so far from Bikini, finally agreed and even sent some men to help Navy Seabees prepare a village there. But events thousands of miles away scuttled that plan. America's weapons designers were pressing for more tests, prompting the new Atomic Energy Commission, which took over the nation's nuclear program from the Army on January 1, 1947, to look for a site better suited than Bikini for a long series of tests.

The search focused on Enewetak Atoll, also part of the Marshall Islands. Unlike at Bikini, the Japanese had fortified Enewetak and defended it in a fierce but short battle in February 1944, forcing the people to flee to the atoll's smaller outlying islands for safety. The

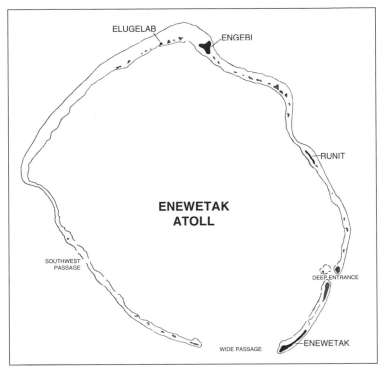

Enewetak Atoll.
WSU Press.

Japanese had built an airstrip on the atoll's biggest island that, with some work, would support traffic for a series of tests.

The Atomic Energy Commission abruptly told the Navy that Enewetak was needed for tests and its people would be moved immediately—to Ujelang, the village prepared for the Bikini people.

So the Navy, desperate by this time and feeling the sting of adverse publicity back home, took the Bikini population to Kwajalein, one of the largest atolls in the Pacific Ocean and the site of a major Navy base. (Even on Kwajalein, the islanders had been moved from the biggest island to smaller islands to make room for the military base.)

On Kwajalein the Bikini people, housed in tents, got plenty of food. But it was only another stop in their exile from Bikini. Within two months, the Bikinians had agreed to move again, to Kili Island in the southern Marshall Islands. During the German colonial period, Kili had been used to produce copra, the oil-bearing meat of the coconut. The island was large enough that the Americans hoped it could support the people, but it lacked a protected lagoon, pretty much ruling out the seafood the people had depended on at Bikini.

Dwight Heine, the first Marshallese appointed district administrator, told me that the stay on Kwajalein was "the worst thing that could have happened" to the Bikinians. The remorseful Americans fed them steak and showed them American movies every night, Heine said, making their adjustment to Kili even more difficult.

The Bikini people are still not home; most are on Kili and on islands at Majuro Atoll, still largely dependent on food from the outside, and still dreaming of an atoll only the older ones remember but one that has changed drastically.

Juda's strong leadership helped hold the community together during years of relocating from Bikini and eventual settlement on Kili Island. There, because the land area was much smaller than at Bikini, he worked out a new system of land ownership, accepted even by those who lost land and influence.

"Juda was sleepy looking and slow talking," Mason said. "A lot of Americans, including me, thought on first meeting him that he wasn't too smart. But when I got to know him I realized he was a strong leader and very able in working out difficult problems."

The Enewetak people's notice that they would be moved from their homes apparently was even more abrupt than at Bikini. The Navy officer told them they would be given a new island and took several leaders to Ujelang Atoll for an inspection. The 120 Enewetak people were moved to Ujelang in December 1947, occupying the village originally intended for the Bikini people.

Ships, construction workers, scientists, and equipment were already heading for Enewetak. Unlike the public spectacle at Bikini, the Enewetak tests beginning in April 1948 were kept secret until the

Participants in the testing at Enewetak are checked for radiation, April and May 1948.
Department of Energy.

first series of three shots was completed. Enewetak's role increased dramatically after the Soviet Union exploded its first atomic bomb in late 1949 and the Cold War's nuclear weapons race began to heat up.

Some of the atoll's islands, once cultivated by the islanders to produce food and copra, were bulldozed for construction of laboratories, offices, barracks, warehouses, mess halls—even two chapels—and a dock to accommodate ocean-going ships. Two quarries produced coral aggregate to make concrete. Coral, seawater, and cement didn't make very good concrete but the alternative was to ship crushed rock thousands of miles.

Over the next ten years, the atoll was the scene of more than 40 nuclear tests, including the first hydrogen bomb, code-named Mike, that destroyed one of the atoll's smaller islands, Elugelab. (Rather than have scientists and workers remember and pronounce Marshallese names, the islands were given code names. Elugelab was Flora.)

A nuclear detonation at Enewetak in 1951.
Department of Energy.

The Enewetak people's new home at Ujelang was smaller than their home atoll—about a quarter the land area and one-fifteenth the lagoon area of Enewetak. It soon became apparent it could not supply enough food or building material for their traditional dwellings and the swift sailing canoes for which they were famous in the islands.

By October of 1967, the food shortage was so acute the people did something unheard of among the Marshallese. When a long-delayed supply ship arrived, many of them swarmed out to the ship in canoes and boarded. They refused to get off and said they would ride back to the district headquarters to protest.

Atoji L. Balos, a Trust Territory officer, talked to them for seven hours as the ship lay in the lagoon. Finally, he promised to stay and "starve with you, if necessary," if they would leave the ship. The people agreed and Balos stayed several weeks until another supply ship made an emergency run to Ujelang with a large amount of food. Unfortunately, because so much food came all at once and there was no refrigeration on the island, much of it spoiled or was eaten by rats.

One year after that protest I spoke with Enewetak leaders who were visiting district headquarters at Majuro. Hertes, 36, the elected magistrate of the people on Ujelang, said the people were short of food again. "The breadfruit and pandanus are out of season," he said. "We can get by when we have them. Our people are also out of rice and flour. They will have to wait until the next ship comes."

"When will that be?" I asked. Hertes shrugged and shook his head. He did not smile.

I inquired about the day the Navy officer asked them to leave their atoll. Johannej, 65, remembered the officer had said America needed the atoll but "we had no idea why they needed Enewetak. We didn't know about the tests until later." He said the officer promised them a new island and a few days later took several men to inspect Ujelang. Johannej recalled telling the officer, "This is no new island. We know this place. It is Ujelang."

America stopped its nuclear-testing program in the Pacific in 1958. Some Enewetak people began returning to their atoll in the 1980s. Half of the land area and much of the lagoon are still radioactively contaminated. The people largely depend on imported food.

Even as American testing remained active at Enewetak, the Soviet Union's emergence as a nuclear power prompted America to expand its testing program, establishing a site in Nevada in 1951. The next year the Atomic Energy Commission, looking for a place to develop the hydrogen bomb (a far more powerful device than it would dare set off in Nevada), decided to reactivate Bikini, which had been neglected since Operation Crossroads in 1946. The new activity at Bikini must have been dismaying to its people, still on Kili Island, still hoping to return home.

The first shot of the renewed program at Bikini, on March 1, 1954, was a 15-megaton hydrogen bomb dubbed Bravo. It was 1,000 times more powerful than the bombs dropped on Japan or the explosion I'd seen in Nevada. It remains the biggest explosion in history, ten times bigger than the Mike blast at Enewetak and apparently more than twice the energy yield expected by the scientists. Add in a flawed weather forecast and Bravo caused human misery and an international controversy.

Forecasters had predicted winds blowing toward the north, which would have carried Bravo's radioactive cloud over 1,000 miles of uninhabited ocean. But the fireball rose 100,000 feet where it reached a wind blowing toward the east, carrying debris toward several inhabited atolls. Scientific and military personnel evacuated from Bikini for the test were on ships 30 miles away where they thought it was safe. But within an hour Geiger counters detected increases in radioactivity on the ships and everyone was ordered below decks.

On the inhabited atoll of Rongelap, 100 miles east of Bikini, people saw a flash and perhaps felt a warm breath of air. A little later, the tremendous whump of the explosion seemed to shake the ground. After several hours, white particles began falling. The people said it looked like snow, which they had heard about but never seen. They had no idea what it was; a few children played with it.

As it turned out, some 200 Marshallese on Rongelap and Utrik Atolls and 28 American military personnel on another island had been exposed to enough radiation that they were taken to the Navy base at Kwajalein for treatment. The Utrik people were able to return in three months, the Rongelap people three years later.

I visited Rongelap in 1964 as a member of a University of Washington group, seven years after the people's return. In a perverse way, they had been lucky. A whim of the wind as Bravo's fallout arrived had delivered a radioactive dose to the main village that doctors describe as one where survival is probable. The uninhabited island of Kabelle, about 20 miles across Rongelap's lagoon, received a dose where human survival would have been unlikely.

Shy, smiling children—the girls in long dresses, the boys in shorts—greeted us on Rongelap's beach as we waded ashore from our small boat. I've wondered since if a boy named Lekoj Anjain was among them. He would have been about 10, the age of some who clustered around us. He was the son of John Anjain, magistrate of Rongelap at the time. During a visit to Rongelap eight years later by American doctors, Lekoj was diagnosed with leukemia, a common result of radiation to children. He would have been one year old when radioactive fallout from the Bravo shot fell at Rongelap. He was taken to America for treatment and died within two months at age 19.

The cemetery at Rongelap.
Courtesy of the author.

On November 23, 1972, I wrote in the *Seattle Times*:

I know the tiny cemetery where they'll be burying Lekoj Anjain in a few days...Lekoj died a week ago in a National Institutes of Health hospital in Bethesda, Md., a little more than 18 years after flaky, white ashes began drifting down on his atoll of Rongelap...

During treatment he developed pneumonia which proved fatal. It's beside the point that Lekoj didn't actually die of leukemia. He still had the tragic distinction of being the world's first victim of H-bomb fallout to develop leukemia.

Lekoj's family in their peaceful island home has one thing to be thankful for. We're not shooting off any more of those things at Bikini.

Unfortunately, the Rongelap people's return in 1957 proved to be temporary. By 1985, human illness and measurements of remaining radioactivity in the environment prompted scientists to recommend another evacuation. Greenpeace sent its ship, the *Rainbow Warrior*, to help move the people to some of the smaller islands of the Kwajalein and Majuro Atolls. They are still there.

In 1996, the United States allocated $45 million toward cleanup of the Rongelap Atoll with the understanding the people would do the job themselves. It seemed a hopeless task with the atoll's 61 islands, some of which needed to have topsoil removed. But Rongelap's leaders say the program is progressing and tourist facilities stressing fishing and diving are in operation. They are optimistic that families will soon begin rebuilding the village.

Another drama that would not come to world attention for two weeks was unfolding the morning of the Bravo explosion even as radioactive material fell on Rongelap. A Japanese tuna-fishing boat, rolling in long swells, its lines out, was about 80 miles east of Bikini. A crewman on deck in the early morning was startled by a sudden yellow glow on the western horizon. Seven minutes later he and other crewmen who had tumbled out of their bunks to watch what seemed like a sunrise in the wrong direction heard the explosion. Ninety minutes later, gritty, snow-like material began falling on the ship.

The crewmen were puzzled. Some tasted the particles to see if they could identify the material. They knew that America had conducted nuclear tests in the Pacific and some wondered if the flash to the west was another test. But it seemed unlikely. The most recent test at Enewetak had been two years before and there had been no tests at Bikini for eight years. Apparently none of them made a connection between a possible test and the strange stuff falling from the sky.

The boat, the *Daigo Fukuryu Maru*, headed for home, a two-week trip. By the third day, crewmen began to experience nausea, burning of the skin, and other symptoms. Even after they left the area they were still being exposed to radiation because, unaware of what the white dust was, they hadn't thoroughly cleaned the ship. The ship's radio operator died two weeks after the ship reached Japan. Doctors said he probably would have survived if medical care had been available during the two-week cruise home.

The *Daigo Fukuryu Maru*'s arrival in Japan caused understandable shock and indignation. Hiroshima and Nagasaki were only nine years in the past. The ship's catch of tuna had been sold before the cause of the crewmen's illness was realized, setting off a search of markets to reclaim it and causing panic among consumers who began to fear fish caught anywhere in the Pacific. The U.S. State Department expressed grave concern "over reports that some Japanese fishermen have suffered injury during the course of atomic tests in the Marshall Islands...despite the careful precautions taken and including warnings issued over a wide area." Actually, the boat, like Rongelap Atoll, had been outside the designated danger zone for the Bravo test. But the surprising size of the explosion and unexpected high-level winds had rendered the danger zone meaningless.

It took months of reassurances by both Japanese and American scientists to calm the panic and restore the Japanese fishery industry.

Juda's grave on Kili Island.
Courtesy of the author.

Chapter 12

Lasting Effects

N ews the Bikini people had been hoping for came in June 1968: *Scientists believe Bikini Atoll, battered by 23 nuclear explosions, is now safe for the people to return.*

The announcement flashed around the world—but not to Kili Island where the Bikini people had lived for 20 years. The generator that powered Kili's community radio was not working.

Todd Jenkins, a Peace Corps volunteer who had been working and living with the Bikini people on Kili for almost a year, heard on his battery-powered radio an urgent call from the Marshall Islands district center at Majuro Atoll: "Kili, call Majuro. Kili, call Majuro." Still, the generator wouldn't start. Three hours later, Jenkins tuned his personal radio to the noon news broadcast from Majuro and heard the spine-tingling news: President Lyndon Johnson had announced that Bikini was now safe; the government would help the people return and begin by taking Bikini leaders for an inspection trip of the atoll.

Jenkins called to the Bikinians to turn on their battery-powered radios and they heard the news repeated in the Marshallese language.

Jenkins expected an emotional outburst at the news. But the Bikini people, although undoubtedly elated, reacted calmly. Jenkins said, "Nothing really happened. Some kids ran around. One pounded a stick on a tree. People smiled quietly. Then it was over."

The official word arrived at Kili a couple of months later, in August, when William R. Norwood, high commissioner for the Trust Territory of the Pacific Islands, arrived at the isolated island. As a reporter for the *Seattle Times*, I accompanied the group. (The United States, which administered the islands under a United Nations mandate after World War II, officially dissolved the Trust Territory in 1986 and the Republic of the Marshall Islands assumed governance.)

Ironically, Norwood, who would officially confirm the news they had been waiting for, arrived in a dumpy little inter-island freighter, outboard boats and tarpaulin-covered mattresses cluttered amidships. Kili Island has no lagoon so the ship, the *James M. Cook*, lowered boats outside the fringing reef. Surf on the reef can be difficult to cross but the wind was calm and the boats got across easily as Bikini men waded out chest deep to escort the visitors. Shy children greeted us on the beach.

Juda, the elected magistrate who had guided the Bikinians into exile, had died of cancer three months before the arrival of the news. Lore (pronounced Lorie), an elder who had replaced him, greeted the visitors: "We heard on the radio but couldn't believe you were coming. Today, we see you as saviors of our people."

Norwood's situation was difficult. He knew the battered Bikini was not ready to take back its people and needed to convey that fact. Speaking to the villagers who sat on white coral gravel in an open space in the village, he warned, "most of the coconuts are gone, some buildings will have to be removed. There are other dangers." He mentioned that money still had to be found to do the job.

Lore's reply was thoughtful. Speaking through an interpreter, he said, "It is the desire of all the Kili people to return to Bikini now. We had thought that all was ready on Bikini. We thought the high commissioner had the necessary budget. However, we will listen to your plan as to the proper way to proceed." Nine Bikini elders would join us for the trip to Bikini.

Before the ship departed, I visited Juda's grave. The cemetery is down a short path at one end of the village, as it was at the old village on Bikini. I wrote in the *Seattle Times* on September 16, 1968:

> The headstone is cut from white coral rock. It was shaped with two axes, two saws and a meat cleaver, which out of respect to the leader must never be used again. Despite the scarcity of tools on Kili, they were tossed into underbrush near the grave where no one will touch them again, where they will rust away to nothing.
>
> The stone says King Juda L., Lotak June 8, 1895, Mij May 4, 1968.

Juda's favorite chair and teapot stand beside the grave which, in the Marshallese custom, is sort of a rock-sided crib built above ground.

Actually, the Bikini people had never called Juda "king." He was the elected magistrate and hereditary head of his clan. The Navy christened him king when they relocated the people and the media adopted it. In small island communities, Marshallese never needed last names but when American paperwork demanded it they used the initial of their father's name.

The next afternoon, as the old ship plodded along on the two-day cruise to Bikini, I joined three of the Bikini elders on deck in the shade of a tarp. We wouldn't sight Bikini until the next morning. There was a cool breeze, a good time to talk. Chuji Chuataro, a 28-year-old Marshallese community development officer with a mainland college degree in sociology, agreed to interpret.

All three—Lore, 60, elected magistrate when Juda died, Kilon, 68, a Bikini councilman, and Jibaj, 69—had been at the fateful meeting with Juda in 1946 when they were asked to leave Bikini. I asked Lore to reconstruct the events leading to their departure. His interpretation of those events, from a vastly different perspective, diverged from the official version.

Lore said a Navy officer told the Bikinians in February that they would be moved in a week. He told them to take a census of the people and count their possessions—houses, coconut trees, canoes, house furnishings, everything.

"We had been counting a week," he continued, "when the Navy admiral came and gathered all the people under the trees in the village. He held up his arms [Lore imitated the gesture] and said: 'I am the only commander here in the Pacific Ocean so what I say no one can change. What I am now telling you is, you move.'"

Lore recalled that Juda had told the officer: "Because you have said it, we will follow what you say. But we do not feel like we want to move." Lore added that the people felt great sorrow, using a Marshallese word that expressed more depth than "sorrow" but for which there is no English equivalent. I asked them other questions:

Why did Juda and other leaders agree so readily? Lore smiled: "The Americans had risked their lives to save us from the Japanese. The officer told us that the purpose of using the islands would be to protect the peace in the world. Besides, according to Marshallese custom, when someone asks you for something, you can't say no."

Did you have any idea how long you would be gone? Kilon: "We didn't know but they told us that right after the bomb test we would be returned, either from a ship far away or from an island."

Did you know how big the bomb would be? Lore: "They told us that the islands would be changed, that they might melt like a bottle. We heard it and we believed it because the Americans said so. But our minds could not absorb it."

Jibaj added that several months after the Bikini people had been moved to Rongerik Atoll, the Navy sent a landing craft, loaded the people, and took them to the middle of the lagoon. They heard a blast and knew what it was.

"We became very angry," Jibaj said, "and then the tears came. We wept because we were afraid it would destroy Bikini." Then, as the Marshallese do when especially sad or lonely, they began to sing.

The blast they heard was the first test on July 1, 1946, the aerial explosion, from 125 miles away. Jibaj didn't know why the Navy took the people out in the lagoon. It may have been a safety measure.

As I began to thank the elders for sharing memories, Chuji nudged me: "Lore has more to say." The Navy officer had told them something else, Lore said. It went something like this:

"We thank Juda and his people for your kindness in offering your land and neglecting your

Lore aboard ship heading for Bikini in 1968.
Courtesy of the author.

own sorrow. You are standing like men, giving the United States your land for the purpose of improving the knowledge of peace in the world. You are like the five virgins in the Bible. You today are the children of the American people. You will be in the book of our generation. You will be the most fortunate human souls on this planet."

Lore paused and then added, "These are the words that Bikinians want to find the answer to."

The next morning, hours before Bikini came in sight, Laijo, 69, was at the ship's bow, his eyes glued to the horizon, the wind whipping his white hair. Lore and several others soon joined him in the watch for Bikini. I dreaded the moment they would get a good look at their islands. I had been there several years before and knew what a mess the testing had left. But these men had not seen Bikini for 22 years, not since the nuclear tests, and must have been remembering it the way it had always been.

The passage through the

Bikini men strained for the first sight of Bikini, 1968.
Courtesy of the author.

reef at the south end of the atoll is shallow, not more than 30 or 40 feet deep. As our ship left the long Pacific Ocean swells and coasted slowly through the channel, the sandy bottom studded with coral was visible through the clear water.

The island on the starboard side was Enyu, the atoll's second biggest after Bikini. Abandoned equipment rusted on the beaches, a 300-foot instrument tower rose above the underbrush, tall metal buildings still stood where the bombs had been assembled, and open spaces, now overgrown, had been bulldozed through what once were groves of coconut trees. What had been smaller islands were now

Bikini men touching their ancestral beach for the first time in 22 years, 1968.
Courtesy of the author.

connected to Enyu by causeways bulldozed over the reef. But if I'd
expected emotion, I was wrong. Their faces were impassive as they
stared silently.

Several hours later we landed on Bikini Island's long, sandy beach,
so white it is almost blinding in the midday sun. On the way in from
the ship in a small boat, the men had directed the helmsman to the
village site with the Marshallese equivalent of "A little to the right.
Too far, back a little. There, you're right on." The Bikini men had
dressed up for the occasion—white shirts, ties, and long trousers.
Some carried their shoes in their hands wading ashore from the small
boat. Again, if I expected drama, I was wrong. Outwardly, they gave
no sign of emotion that their bare feet were sinking into ancestral
land for the first time after such a long hiatus.

They walked silently in single file the short distance up the beach
to where the village had been, now overgrown. Norwood had brought
two flagpoles to be erected for American and Marshallese flags. The
Bikinians wanted them at the village cemetery, which could have been
a problem because Americans had been unable to find the overgrown
graveyard in previous visits over the years.

But the Bikini men almost immediately pointed out coral head-stones. It must have been a sentimental moment but instead of showing it they fell to with machetes, clearing a space for the flagpoles. The flags went up, but perhaps more significantly a few sprouted coconuts were planted near the poles. Coconuts, an economic mainstay of the islands, had been all but wiped out by the testing.

Three of us hacked our way through underbrush from the lagoon side to the ocean reef and sat down to rest in the oppressive heat. Mojej, the community judge, joined us. His eyes were shining as he pointed, "My land." He showed us the boundary, invisible to American eyes, between his and his neighbor's property. There was only one coconut tree there, a survivor of the blasts. Mojej climbed it and threw down drinking nuts for the guests on his land.

For several days the old *James M. Cook* steamed slowly around the atoll, giving the Bikini men opportunities to go ashore. Off one island one pointed and said, "That is Lore's land." Lore said nothing then or later ashore on his island when he climbed a massive concrete bunker used to shield instruments and looked it over impassively.

Namu is one of the larger islands across the lagoon from Bikini. A huge hole interrupts the reef next to Namu, the crater blasted out by the Bravo superbomb, the most powerful explosion ever in the world. There once were two small islands next to Namu.

I was with three Bikini men on Namu's rocky beach as they looked across to the deep blue crater. Kilon, whose family had owned the destroyed islands, turned away so the others would not see his tears, a rare display of emotion for the Marshallese.

On the cruise back to Kili from Bikini, Norwood convened a morning meeting on the ship's foredeck to tell the Bikini men what he could of the future. On September 19, 1968, I wrote in the *Seattle Times*:

> Getting the work started depends on money, he explained, and money depends on developing a plan. "The government will want to know why there is a need to put Bikini back in use," Norwood told the men who had given their land to the same government 22 years before.
>
> "It is very difficult to say when anyone can go back. But we all believe we should start as soon as we can."

As usual, the eloquence was from Lore. He began by a careful enumeration of the damaged islands.

"On the northern part of the atoll there were four islands where we made copra. Today there is not a tree and parts of the islands have disappeared. On Namu there are no edible plants and part of the island is gone. With three islands near it, the same story." His quiet voice went on in a careful, restrained summary of the atoll's condition.

"What we have seen has made us sad." He said it followed the sad story of their exile on Kili Island. "But we want to cooperate. Please tell us what you have in mind for Bikini."

Norwood apologetically said he didn't know. "All I can offer," he said, "is our determination to do all we can."

Lore concluded sincerely: "Thank you for your kindness and hospitality. We patiently wait."

The meeting broke up and the Americans trooped down a ladder to breakfast. The Bikini men remained on deck, staring thoughtfully at the sea.

The trip had failed in one important respect. A purpose had been to enlist the aid of the Bikini people in developing a plan for their atoll. This had not happened...Norwood had said only: "The Trust Territory government is going to prepare a redevelopment plan... We'll keep you informed."

Something Lore said on another day came to mind: "When the Americans first came to the islands you smelled like the sweetest flower we ever had smelled. But when you left us after the tests, your image was like footprints on the beach after the waves had washed over them."

Some rehabilitation work began in the years after the hopeful visit of the Bikini leaders in 1968. Replanting of coconut trees was largely complete by 1972. But warnings by American scientists that some foods on the atoll were still not safe to eat caused the Bikini Council to vote not to return as a community but to leave it up to individual families to make the decision. Several extended families moved back to Bikini in 1972 along with a crew of Marshallese workmen who continued rehabilitation of the islands. Unfortunately, by 1975 radioactivity levels in food and water caused concern and the families left Bikini again.

Beginning in the mid-1990s, the Bikini Council ran a diving business at the atoll, offering the rare opportunity of exploring sunken warships on the lagoon bottom. The diving received rave reviews, the accommodations were comfortable, and the food was imported and safe. But the activity was suspended after a year or so because of rising fuel costs and unpredictable airline transportation to the atoll. A few maintenance workers were the only inhabitants in 2010.

Nuclear testing ended in 1958 at both Bikini and Enewetak Atolls. Before it ended, America crowded an astounding 20-plus nuclear tests at or near Enewetak in less than four months in 1958. Today, such an intense program—averaging more than one shot a week—is almost unbelievable. But we should remember the United States was in a nuclear-arms race with the Soviet Union in those years. Undoubtedly contributing to the rush to perform as many tests as possible was the imminence of a testing moratorium, put in place because of increasing public concern over health hazards of atmospheric fallout. Indeed, on October 31, 1958, the Eisenhower administration announced a unilateral cessation of nuclear tests. This moratorium by the United States, although suspended off and on a few times in the first years, eventually led to the situation today, where nuclear tests are rare rather than routine.

The first of that last series of tests, lifted by a balloon, detonated 86,000 feet above the ocean about 90 miles northeast of Enewetak on April 28. The next three months saw tests on islands, on barges, and underwater. The last shot at Enewetak was August 18, 1958.

Enewetak continued in use for other military purposes through the 1960s. The atoll was a target area for test rockets fired from Vandenberg Air Base in California. Rocket engines were tested on one of the islands, scorching nearby areas. And what the military called cratering tests—a study of the holes blasted by conventional explosives—left some of the islands pockmarked with smaller craters.

The United States announced in 1972 that it would return the Enewetak people to their atoll, and began a cleanup in 1977 involving thousands of G.I.s and costing more than $1 million.

One of the gaping craters blasted out of an island during that last series played a role in the cleanup. A nuclear device code-named Cactus—1,432 pounds, 69 inches long, and 18 inches in diameter—had been detonated on the surface of Runit Island on the eastern rim of the atoll on May 5, 1958. Its energy yield, equivalent to 18,000 tons of TNT, blasted out a steep-sided crater 350 feet in diameter, 37 feet deep, and ringed by a lip from 8 to 14 feet high.

Today the Cactus Crater is the tomb for more than 110,000 cubic yards of radioactively contaminated soil scraped from six of the atoll's southerly islands, the ones deemed fit for rehabilitation and human occupation.

The whole mess of scraped soil, along with the junk that had littered the southern islands, was barged across the lagoon to Runit Island, mixed in cement slurry, and dumped into Cactus Crater. The mounded pile of waste was covered with 358 huge concrete panels,

Twin craters at the north end of Runit Island. Cactus Crater, lower, was filled with radioactive debris and capped with concrete. The other crater is in the reef.
Google Earth.

18 inches thick, making a dome more than 370 feet in diameter and almost 30 feet high.

I was on Runit Island in 1964—years before the cleanup began—and climbed the lip around Cactus Crater to peer inside. Water filled the bottom. A University of Washington scientist slid down the crater's steep sides to scrape samples of algae from rocks and collect bits of coral. He was surprised at the growth inside the crater six years after the blast. He saved the samples for testing of radioactive concentrations. Elsewhere on the island sparse vegetation was making a comeback, but the ground around Cactus Crater was bare and gravelly. It looked like something on the moon.

The island and the reef on the ocean side were littered with wreckage from the tests—twisted steel, damaged concrete structures. I could see a large dark-blue area on the reef. It marked a crater a little bigger and deeper than Cactus. It resulted from a shot in 1956, detonated on a barge. Aerial photos show the craters, almost side by side.

The end of the island near Cactus was pocked with small craters, 20 feet or so in diameter. Pre-World War II Runit Island had been a thriving coconut plantation, with trees tended by the Enewetak people for copra production.

Today there are signs warning against landing on Runit Island. It is possible to ignore the warnings and climb the massive dome. Brief visits are not particularly dangerous. You probably wouldn't want to live near it.

Some of the Enewetak people moved home in 1980 but not to the atoll they remembered. It was a battered, only partly restored, Enewetak. About 8 percent of the atoll's land area had disappeared. Less than half of the remaining land was deemed safe for rehabilitation and occupation. Food is mostly imported from outside the atoll.

Runit Island, the former coconut plantation, was out of bounds for resettlement, of course, as was Engebi, a large island on the atoll's north rim where part of the Enewetak community had once lived. Even before the nuclear tests, Engebi was battered during World War II. The Japanese had bulldozed an airfield straight across the triangular-shaped island and built a pier for small craft on the lagoon side of the island. The weeklong battle when Americans took the island in 1944 knocked down most of the trees. Nuclear tests in the 1950s added to the damage.

There were still spent cartridge casings, mostly rifle, on the beach when I was on Engebi Island in 1964. I walked to a three-story concrete blockhouse built for a 1952 nuclear test. The damage was awesome. Heavy steel girders were twisted. One section of heavy reinforced concrete was pushed about 15 feet away from the structure and fell one story. Tiles were shattered, sheet metal peeled back. But nature had moved in. Vegetation had rooted in rubble on the second and third floors of the pushed-out section. One messerschmidia (a shrubby tree) was 15 feet tall.

Of the 167 persons who left Bikini in 1946, less than 40 were still living in 2010. Those who were very young when they left know the atoll only through their parents' stories.

With births and marriages to people of other islands, the number of Bikinians has increased to about 4,000, most of them on Kili Island, Majuro Atoll, and other Marshall Islands. Several hundred live in the United States. Obviously, Bikini Atoll could not support those numbers, even if they all wanted to return. After all these years, many would not want to. Few today remember the subsistence economy of pre-World War II days. New ideas and new blood have been introduced by young people who have attended schools on other islands and by spouses who have married into the group.

Most of those who visited Bikini in 1968 with the hope they could move back have died: Lore in 1994, age 86; Kilon in 1992, age 92; Jibaj in 1984, age 85; and Laijo in 1984, age 85. They are buried on Kili Island.

Juda, who died at age 72 only months before that hopeful 1968 visit, requested that if his people were ever able to return to their home atoll, his remains be reburied in the old village cemetery on Bikini. His grave is still on Kili Island.

Efforts for compensation

The effort by people of the Marshall Islands to be compensated for damages caused by the testing program has a long and complicated history:

1979 The Marshall Islands became self-governing. Three years later it adopted the name Republic of the Marshall Islands.

1982 The peoples of Bikini, Enewetak, Rongelap, and Utrik Atolls filed claims with the U.S. Court of Federal Claims for compensation of damages, loss of use of their land, and the hardships of evacuation.

1983 Marshall Island voters approved a Compact of Free Association with the United States, a pact approved by the U.S. Congress in 1986. The compact established a Nuclear Claims Tribunal with "jurisdiction to render final determination upon all claims past, present and future... related to the Nuclear Testing Program."

This meant the claimants had to start over. The U.S. Court of Federal Claims ruled it no longer had jurisdiction because the Tribunal was responsible for deciding compensation amounts and awarding funds. The U.S. Court of Appeals upheld the ruling. But, importantly, neither ruling disputed U.S. obligations to compensate for damages from the tests.

The compact also established a $150 million trust fund, money provided by the United States, with proceeds to be used for rehabilitation of the atolls over 15 years. During that time the Nuclear Claims Tribunal "awarded" more than $1 billion in claims, mostly for property damage and some for personal injury. But the awards, far exceeding available funds, were largely meaningless.

2000 The Marshall Islands government requested the U.S. Congress cover unpaid Tribunal claims.

2001 The compact expired. The Marshall Islands' request to negotiate a compact extension was rejected because the funding issue was before Congress.

2006 The people of Bikini and Enewetak returned to the U.S. Court of Federal Claims. The claims were dismissed as premature because the 2000 request was still before Congress.

2007 Senate Bill 1756 was introduced in the U.S. Senate. It would have provided $4.5 million annually through 2023 to provide health care and monitoring for people of the four affected atolls; provide funds for monitoring radioactivity in the soil, water, and marine life near the Runit Island dome; and make Marshallese who worked as contract employees of the U.S. Department of Energy at the Bikini and Enewetak sites eligible for the same benefits as U.S. citizens who work at nuclear-cleanup sites.

2008 Senate Bill 1756 died.

2010 The Republic of the Marshall Islands asked that a bill similar to S-1756 be introduced in the U.S. Congress. The Marshallese say their claims are a tiny fraction of the billions of dollars the United States spent on the tests and more billions being spent on nuclear-cleanup sites in the United States.

After the Bomb

Niels Bohr organized the first Atoms for Peace Conference in Geneva in 1955. He died in Copenhagen in 1962 at age 77.

Walther Bothe shared the Nobel Prize in physics in 1954. He died in Heidelberg in 1957 at age 66.

Vannevar Bush continued as president of the Carnegie Institute until 1955. He served on several government boards and from 1957 to 1962 was chairman of the pharmaceutical firm Merck & Co. He died in Massachusetts in 1974 at age 84.

James Chadwick returned to England and was elected master of Gonville and Caius College, Cambridge, retiring in 1959. He was a member of the United Kingdom Atomic Energy Authority from 1957 to 1962. He died in 1974 at age 82.

Arthur H. Compton was chancellor of Washington University in St. Louis from 1946 until 1953 but remained on the faculty until 1961. He died in California in 1962, at age 69.

James B. Conant served as Harvard University president until 1953. He was ambassador to Germany from 1953 until 1957 and served as advisor to the National Science Foundation and the Atomic Energy Commission. He died in New Hampshire in 1978 at age 84.

Lauren R. Donaldson directed the University of Washington's Laboratory of Radiation Biology, which monitored radiation levels at the Pacific testing sites, and continued as professor of fisheries. He died in Seattle in 1998 at age 95.

Enrico Fermi became an American citizen in 1944 and two years later joined the University of Chicago's Institute for Nuclear Studies. He died in Chicago in 1954 at age 53 of cancer caused by heavy radiation exposure.

James Franck was named professor emeritus at the University of Chicago in 1947 but continued as head of the university's photosynthesis-research group until 1956. He died in 1964 at age 71 during a visit to the University of Gottingen in Germany, where he had taught in the 1920s and 1930s.

Otto Frisch returned to England in 1946 to join the Atomic Energy Research Establishment. He taught at Cambridge until 1972 and died there in 1979 at age 74.

Crawford H. Greenewalt was president of DuPont from 1948 to 1962. Combining his interests in photography and birds, he published books on hummingbirds in 1960 and 1968. He died in Delaware in 1993 at age 91.

Brig. Gen. Leslie R. Groves retired from the Army in 1949 and was a vice president of the Sperry Rand Corp. until 1961. He died in Washington, D.C., in 1970 at age 73.

William L. Laurence was born Leib W. Siew in Lithuania, then part of Russia, and changed his name when he moved to the United States in 1905. As science writer for the *New York Times*, he was "drafted" to be the historian for the Manhattan Project and was the only journalist to witness the nuclear test in New Mexico and the bombing of Nagasaki. He returned to the *Times* after the war and retired in 1964. He died in 1977 in Spain at age 89.

Ernest O. Lawrence became active in efforts to halt testing of nuclear bombs and was attending a 1958 conference on that subject in Geneva when he became ill and returned home. He died in California a month later at age 57.

Leona (Woods) Marshall Libby returned to academics. After she and John Marshall divorced, she married Willard Libby, winner of a Nobel Prize in chemistry. She was a defender of nuclear energy during controversy over its safety in the 1970s and 1980s. She died in California in 1986 at age 67.

Leonard Mason continued working with the Bikini people and helped found the University of Hawaii's program in Pacific Island

Studies. He headed the anthropology department for many years, retiring from the university in 1969. He died in 2005 at age 92.

Lt. Col. Franklin T. Matthias was awarded the Distinguished Service Medal for his work at Hanford. After construction work in Brazil and Canada, he joined Kaiser Engineers as a vice president in 1960 and retired in 1973. He died in California in 1993 at age 85.

Lise Meitner, Otto Hahn, and **Fritz Strassmann** shared the Enrico Fermi Award in 1966. Meitner died in England in 1968 at age 89. Twenty-nine years after her death, the man-made element 109 was named meitnerium in her honor. Hahn died in 1968 at age 89 and Strassmann died in 1980 at age 78, both in Germany.

Col. Kenneth D. Nichols retired from the Army as a major general in 1953 and served as general manager of the Atomic Energy Commission until 1955. He then established a consulting firm specializing in atomic energy research and development. He died in Maryland in 2000 at age 92.

Jack Niedenthal, who grew up in Pennsylvania, went to the Marshall Islands as a Peace Corps volunteer in 1981. He has lived and worked with the people of Bikini since 1984.

Ida Noddack, who continued research in chemistry in Germany until retiring in 1968, received the High Service Cross of the Federal Republic of Germany in 1966. She died in Germany in 1978 at age 82.

J. Robert Oppenheimer, director of the secret laboratory in Los Alamos, New Mexico, became director of the Institute for Advanced Study in Princeton, New Jersey, in 1947. Allegations of associations with communists during the war years resulted in his being stripped of his security clearance in 1953. Ten years later, in a gesture of rehabilitation, he was awarded the Enrico Fermi Award. He died in 1967 at age 62.

Glenn T. Seaborg was chancellor of the University of California at Berkeley from 1958 to 1961 and served as chairman of the Atomic Energy Commission, the predecessor of the Department of Energy, from 1961 to 1971. He died in California in 1999 at age 86.

Emilio Segrè became a citizen in 1944 and remained at Berkeley after the war. He died in California in 1989 at age 84.

Leo Szilard changed his research to molecular biology after the war and died in California in 1964 at age 66.

John A. Wheeler was at Princeton University until he reached mandatory retirement age in 1976 and moved to the University of Texas. Active into his 90s, he coined the term black hole. He died in New Jersey in 2008 at age 96.

Hill Williams Sr. was the editor and publisher of the weekly *Pasco Herald* during Hanford's construction years. Failing health prompted him to sell the business in 1946. He died in 1948 at age 54. His wife, **Ursula Trainor Williams**, worked at the *Herald* during the war years and later was women's editor of the daily *Tri-City Herald*. She retired in 1964 and died in 1967 at age 74.

Concerned Scientists:
The Franck Report

By 1944, hard-nosed engineering was transforming esoteric nuclear theory into concrete and steel at Hanford. The B Reactor, rising incongruously above the desert and nearby river, was nearing completion.

Not surprisingly, the scientific workload at the Metallurgical Laboratory in Chicago had dropped significantly. Scientists, whose long hours and brainpower had provided the wherewithal to convert theory into blueprints, had time to think about the future of atomic energy and how the bomb would be used.

Defeat of the German Army's last major offensive in the Battle of the Bulge made Germany's surrender seem imminent; discussions in the still-secret Met Lab turned to whether the bomb should be used against Japan. Arthur Compton, the lab director (perhaps recalling the near rebellion of the lab scientists when the Army and DuPont assumed leadership of the project), suggested the scientists put their ideas on paper.

James Franck, 62, director of the lab's chemistry division, began collecting and recording the concerns. Winner of a 1925 Nobel Prize, Franck was probably the most prestigious scientist at the lab.

It was a crucial time—the world on the verge of the nuclear age, the public still completely unaware—as Franck compiled his colleagues' concerns into a document that became known as the Franck Report. Perhaps it would be useful to take a moment to consider this moment in history, the spring of 1945:

- President Roosevelt died April 12, leaving responsibility for the new weapon with his successor, Harry S. Truman, who only then learned of the bomb project. A month later Truman approved formation of a secret interim committee to study policy problems of the new form of energy and, specifically, how the bomb should be used.

- Germany surrendered on May 7, and it became apparent that their atomic research lagged well behind the United States. There was also no significant concern that Japan was trying to build one.

- No one was certain that either of America's bomb designs would really work, particularly the one armed with plutonium produced at Hanford. (The test of a plutonium device in New Mexico did not take place until July 16.)

- Incendiary bombing had reduced Japan's major cities to ashes, with great loss of life. The Army Air Corps, with control of the air over Japan, believed continued bombing would force surrender. The Navy, which controlled the sea around the Japanese islands, maintained that cutting off supplies would starve Japan into surrendering.

- Japan had secretly asked the Soviet Union to act as a broker in a possible peace arrangement, one that would preserve the emperor. (America, which had broken the Japanese code, knew of this diplomatic move.) But the Japanese military continued to defy demands from America and Britain for unconditional surrender, a demand the Japanese feared would eliminate the emperor.

- The conquest of Okinawa, completed in mid-June, had been one of the most costly—in numbers of both American and Japanese lives—of any battle in World War II. It was assumed that an invasion of the main Japanese islands would be even more costly.

- American lives were being lost every day in the Pacific, adding pressure to end the war as quickly as possible. Veterans of the European campaign were being deployed to the Pacific. America's joint chiefs ordered preparation of plans for an invasion of the island of Kyushu, to begin in November.

This was the situation in the spring of 1945 as Franck finished the report, signed by seven Met Lab scientists, among them Franck, Glenn Seaborg, and Leo Szilard.

"It is not at all certain," the report said, "that American public opinion, if it could be enlightened as to the effect of atomic explosives, would approve of our own country being the first to introduce such an indiscriminate method of wholesale destruction of civilian life."

The report urged that the first use of a bomb be announced in advance and be conducted as a public demonstration on a "desert or a barren island…After such a demonstration the weapon could be used against Japan if a sanction of the United Nations (and of the public opinion at home) could be obtained, perhaps after a preliminary ultimatum to Japan to surrender or at least to evacuate a certain region as an alternative to the total destruction of this target."

The report tried to explain why scientists who developed the weapon with all possible speed "would be reluctant to try it out on the enemy as soon as it is available." Their motivation, the report continued, had been "the certainty that German scientists were working on this weapon and that their government would certainly have no scruples against using it when available."

Met Lab scientists urged Franck to personally take the report to Washington, D.C. Compton tried to get an appointment for Franck to see Henry Stimson, secretary of war and chairman of the interim committee, but Stimson was out of town. The report went to a Stimson aide on June 12.

The interim committee referred the report to its scientific advisory panel, which considered it on June 16. The panel concluded: "we can propose no technical demonstration likely to bring an end to the war; we see no acceptable alternative to direct military use." Panel members were Compton, Ernest O. Lawrence (of Cal's Radiation Laboratory), Robert Oppenheimer (director of the bomb-assembly laboratory at Los Alamos), and Enrico Fermi.

The scientific panel apparently did not reconsider the Franck Report after the July 16 test of the plutonium bomb in New Mexico when the enormity of its force was better understood.

There were several arguments against a public bomb demonstration. If the Japanese knew the timing and location they might try to shoot down the bomber—or move American prisoners of war into the target area. If the bomb was a dud, nuclear material might fall into Japanese hands—not a very impressive demonstration. And sampling American opinion and notifying the United Nations—still in the process of being formed—about a top-secret project would be nearly impossible.

Opinions among the Met Lab scientists were mixed after the interim committee did not respond to the Franck Report. A poll at the lab showed that 15 percent of the scientists favored military use of the bomb to bring a quick surrender and save American lives. Only 2 percent were flatly against use of the bomb. Most of the other votes were for a range of options for some type of demonstration before giving Japan an opportunity to surrender.

The soul-searching scientists at Met Lab may or may not have known another critical factor: the actual explosive for the bombs was in extremely short supply. Hanford was shipping every bit of plutonium it could manufacture to the bomb makers preparing to test the implosion device in New Mexico. The huge plant at Oak Ridge was straining to produce enough enriched uranium for a first bomb. Material for a second uranium bomb would not have been in hand for weeks.

As spring became summer 1945, Szilard tried another approach—a direct appeal to Truman, circulating petitions asking the president "to rule that the United States shall not resort to the use of atomic bombs in this war unless the terms which will be imposed upon Japan have been made public in detail and Japan knowing these terms has refused to surrender."

Szilard sent petitions to Oak Ridge and Los Alamos, both much busier places than the Met Lab. The petitions were not circulated at Los Alamos or apparently at Hanford, where the emphasis was on engineering and where few knew what they were actually working on.

Compton delivered Szilard's petition, with more than 100 signatures from the Met Lab and Oak Ridge, to Washington on July 19.

With delays moving through the chain of command, the petition finally reached Stimson's office on August 1. President Truman was at the Potsdam Conference in Germany with Churchill and Stalin and didn't return to Washington until August 7, the day after the Hiroshima bombing. He apparently never saw Szilard's petition.

Existence of the Franck Report remained secret until it was published on May 1, 1946, in the *Bulletin of the Atomic Scientists*.

Bibliography

Alperovitz, Gar. *The Decision to Use the Atomic Bomb and the Architecture of an American Myth.* New York: Vintage Books, 1996.

Bernstein, Jeremy. *Plutonium: A History of the World's Most Dangerous Element.* Washington, D.C.: Joseph Henry Press, 2007.

Compton, Arthur Holly. *Atomic Quest: A Personal Narrative.* New York: Oxford University Press, 1956.

Feis, Herbert. *Japan Subdued: The Atomic Bomb and the End of the War in the Pacific.* Princeton: Princeton University Press, 1961.

Gephart, Roy E. *Hanford: A Conversation about Nuclear Waste and Cleanup.* Columbus, Ohio: Battelle Press, 2003.

Gerber, Michele Stenehjem. *On the Home Front: The Cold War Legacy of the Hanford Nuclear Site.* Lincoln: University of Nebraska Press, 1992.

Groves, Leslie R. *Now It Can Be Told: The Story of the Manhattan Project.* New York: Harper, 1962.

Hershberg, James G. *James B. Conant: Harvard to Hiroshima and the Making of the Nuclear Age.* New York: Knopf, 1993.

Hevly, Bruce, and John M. Finley, eds. *The Atomic West.* Seattle: University of Washington Press, 1998.

Hines, Neal O. *Proving Ground: An Account of the Radiobiological Studies in the Pacific, 1946-1961.* Seattle: University of Washington Press, 1962.

Jones, Vincent C. *Manhattan: The Army and the Atomic Bomb.* Washington, D.C.: Center of Military History, U.S. Army, 1985.

Jungk, Robert. *Brighter than a Thousand Suns: A Personal History of the Atomic Scientists.* New York: Harcourt Brace, 1958.

Kiste, Robert C. *The Bikinians: A Study in Forced Migration.* Menlo Park, California: Cummings, 1974.

_____. *Kili Island: A Study of the Relocation of the Ex-Bikini Marshallese.* Eugene: Department of Anthropology, University of Oregon, 1968.

Laurence, William L. *Dawn Over Zero: The Story of the Atomic Bomb.* Westport, Connecticut: Greenwood Press, 1972.

_____. *Men and Atoms: The Discovery, the Uses, and the Future of Atomic Energy.* New York: Simon & Schuster, 1959.

Lawren, William. *The General and the Bomb: A Biography of General Leslie R. Groves, Director of the Manhattan Project.* New York: Dodd, Mead, 1988.

Libby, Leona Marshall. *The Uranium People.* New York: Crane, Russak, 1979.

Marceau, Thomas E., David W. Harvey, Darby C. Stapp, Sandra D. Cannon, Charles A. Conway, Dennis H. Deford, Brian J. Freer, Michele S. Gerber, Joy K. Keating, Christine F. Noonan, and Gene Weisskopf. *Hanford Site Historic District: History of the Plutonium Production Facilities 1943-1990.* Columbus, Ohio: Battelle Press, 2003.

McKay, Alwyn. *The Making of the Atomic Age.* Oxford: Oxford University Press, 1984.

Nichols, Kenneth D. *The Road to Trinity: A Personal Account of How America's Nuclear Policies Were Made.* New York: Morrow, 1987.

Niedenthal, Jack. *For the Good of Mankind: A History of the People of Bikini and Their Islands.* Majuro, Marshall Islands: Bravo Publishers, 2001.

Norris, Robert S. *Racing for the Bomb: General Leslie R. Groves, the Manhattan Project's Indispensable Man.* South Royalton, Vermont: Steerforth Press, 2002.

Oberst, Walter A. *Railroads, Reclamation and the River: A History of Pasco.* Pasco: Franklin County Historical Society, 1978.

Preston, Diana. *Before the Fallout: From Marie Curie to Hiroshima.* New York: Walker, 2005.

Rhodes, Richard. *The Making of the Atomic Bomb.* New York: Simon & Schuster, 1988.

Sanger, S.L. *Working on the Bomb: An Oral History of WW II Hanford.* Portland: Continuing Education Press, Portland State University, 1995.

Seaborg, Glenn T. *Adventures in the Atomic Age: From Watts to Washington.* With Eric Seaborg. New York: Farrar, Straus and Giroux, 2001.

Kathren, Ronald L., Jerry B. Gough, and Gary T. Benefiel, eds. *The Plutonium Story: The Journals of Professor Glenn T. Seaborg 1939-1946.* Columbus, Ohio: Battelle Press, 1994.

Segrè, Emilio. *Enrico Fermi: Physicist.* Chicago: University of Chicago Press, 1970.

Smyth, Henry D. *Atomic Energy for Military Purposes: The Official Report on the Development of the Atomic Bomb under the Auspices of the United States Government, 1940-1945.* Princeton: Princeton University Press, 1945.

Sweeney, Michael S. *Secrets of Victory: The Office of Censorship and the American Press and Radio in World War II.* Chapel Hill: University of North Carolina Press, 2001.

Tobin, J.A. *The Bikini People: Past and Present.* Majuro, Marshall Islands. Unpublished. 1953.

Wheeler, John Archibald. *Geons, Black Holes and Quantum Foam: A Life in Physics.* With Kenneth Ford. New York: Norton, 1998.

Zachary, G. Pascal. *Endless Frontier: Vannevar Bush, Engineer of the American Century.* New York: Free Press, 1997.

Index

separation plant. *See* "Queen Mary"
Sieg, Lee Paul, 121
silver, 91
Simon, Walter O., 98
Skartland, Olav, 85
Smith, B.B., 86, 93
Smyth, Henry D., 142
Smyth report, 39, 142
Soviet Union, xv, 20, 65, 119, 122,
    142, 151, 153, 167, 178
Stalin, Joseph, xv, 181
Stimson, Henry, 83–84, 139, 179, 181
Stoffel, Karl, 92
Strassmann, Fritz, 28–29, 34, 37, 175
Swing, Joseph, 136
Szilard, Leo, xiii, 25–26, 31–32,
    39, 48, 57–60, 64, 69, 75, 176,
    179–81

T
Tennessee, 11, 15, 74, 99, 110,
    126–27, 130, 139–40
Thompson, Stan, 72
Thompson, William F., 121
Three Mile Island, 119
tickling the dragon's tail, 131
Tobin, Jack A., 146
tritium, 47
Truman, Harry S., xv, 83–85, 139,
    177–78, 180–81
    Committee, 83, 85
Turner, Louis, 48

U
Ujelang, 148–50, 152–53
United Nations, 159, 179–80
United States, xiii, xvi, 31, 62, 65,
    136, 138, 143, 156, 159, 163,
    167–68, 170–72, 174, 178, 180

uranium
    bomb, xv, 52, 56, 61, 131, 180
    bombarding with neutrons, 28,
        34–35, 44, 46–47, 52–54, 58,
        71, 74, 94
    committee, 48, 52, 56, 60–61, 63
    as fuel, 79, 97, 100, 102–3, 105–7,
        111–12, 116–17
    metal scarcity, 60, 64–65, 100
    as tamper, 128–29
    as target in gun assembly,
        126–27, 130–31
    uranium-235, 46–48, 52–56, 58,
        60–61, 66, 68, 74, 76, 94, 100,
        130–1, 140
    uranium-238, 22–23, 46–48,
        52–54, 56–57, 60, 68
    uranium-239, 52–53, 55
Utrik Atoll, xvi, 154, 171

W
Wahl, Arthur C., 51
waste storage, liquid, 93, 118–19
Wheeler, John A., xiii, 42–49, 57, 94,
    98–102, 176
White Bluffs, 4, 10, 13, 18, 70, 92
White, Compton I., 84–85
Wigner, Eugene, 48, 69, 75, 100,
    110–11
Williams, Hill, Sr., 3–7, 19, 87, 91–92,
    140, 176
Williams, Ursula Trainor, 19–20,
    141, 176
Wilmington, Delaware, 16, 19,
    78, 105
Wilson, Bob, 75
Wyatt, Ben H., 144

X
xenon-135, 99–100, 102